VOLUME 31, NUMBER 1, JUNE 2022

qui parle

CRITICAL HUMANITIES AND SOCIAL SCIENCES

Editors in Chief
Zachary Hicks and Kyra Sutton
University of California, Berkeley

Published by
Duke University Press

T0324269

Qui Parle invites submissions from a range of fields, including but not limited to

Aesthetics	History
Anthropology	Literary and Cultural Studies
Critical Race Studies	Philosophy
Critical Theory	Political Theory
Gender and Sexuality Studies	Religion

Submissions of essays and book reviews may be sent directly to the editors at

Qui Parle
Doreen B. Townsend Center for the Humanities
220 Stephens Hall, #2340
University of California, Berkeley
Berkeley, CA 94720-2340
Phone: 510-643-0737
Fax: 510-643-5284
Email: quiparlejournal@gmail.com
Website: quiparle.berkeley.edu

Qui Parle (ISSN: 1041-8385) is published twice a year by Duke University Press, 905 W. Main St., Suite 18B, Durham, NC 27701. It is an interdisciplinary journal that publishes works across the humanities and social sciences. *Qui Parle* is edited by graduate students at the University of California, Berkeley, and sponsored by the Doreen B. Townsend Center for the Humanities.

Direct all orders to Duke University Press, Journals Customer Relations, 905 W. Main St., Suite 18B, Durham, NC 27701. Annual subscription rates: print-plus-electronic institutions, $150; print-only institutions, $132; e-only institutions, $118; individuals, $42; students, $25. For information on subscriptions to the e-Duke Journals Scholarly Collections, contact libraryrelations@dukeupress .edu. Print subscriptions: add $8 postage and applicable HST (including 5% GST) for Canada; add $10 postage outside the US and Canada. Back volumes (institutions): $132. Single issues: institutions, $66; individuals, $12. For more information, contact Duke University Press Journals at 888-651-0122 (toll-free in the US and Canada) or 919-688-5134; subscriptions@dukeupress.edu.

Direct inquiries about advertising to Journals Advertising Coordinator, journals_advertising@dukeupress.edu.

Visit Duke University Press Journals at dukeupress.edu/journals.

For a list of the sources in which *Qui Parle* is indexed and abstracted, see dukeupress.edu/qui-parle.

Qui Parle is grateful to Teresa Stojkov and Anthony Cascardi at the Doreen B. Townsend Center for the Humanities at the University of California, Berkeley, whose continued generosity and support have made publication of the journal possible.

Qui Parle is published by Duke University Press on behalf of the journal's Editorial Board.

ISSN 1041-8385

Contents

Introduction

The Paranormative

EDITORIAL BOARD

Over two years later, a "return to normal" remains the pandemic's most enduring political promise, a token of hope to hedge against continued death and precarity. Held within this recursive promise, however, is a prima facie condition that deserves interrogation. What, exactly, is the "normal" to which we will return? Will capitalism and its attendant crises no longer demand our attention absent a continual state of emergency? The coherence and stability of the "normal" eludes us. Georges Canguilhem sees the normal as itself a chimeric category that, from the perspective of medicine and science, is not so distant from the "pathological" it is meant to foil.

In the contemporary moment, what we might term *paranormativity* has further infringed on our so-called norms, unfolding in internet circles, blue-chip art institutions, and scenes of communal mourning. We need look only to the ascendance of #Witchtok, the surge of astrology apps, and the recent proliferation of art programming such as *Hilma af Klint: Paintings for the Future* (2018), *Agnes Pelton: Desert Transcendentalist* (2019), and *Another World: The Transcendental Painting Group* (2021), among many others, to get a sense of this

QUI PARLE Vol. 31, No. 1, June 2022
DOI 10.1215/10418385-9669448 © 2022 Editorial Board, *Qui Parle*

phenomenon. With the popular renewal of astrological, mystical, and pagan practices and discourses, we are witnessing a contemporary cultural demand for paranormal knowledge that exceeds the epistemological limitations of the secular. In recent years much critical attention has been directed toward traversing these limitations, as evidenced by recuperations of metaphysics and studies of non-Western approaches to knowledge. Scholars such as M. Jacqui Alexander, Jeffrey Sconce, Omise'eke Natasha Tinsley, Harry Garuba, and Jefferey Kripal, among many others, have helped shape a field that resists the transformation of the paranormal into a symbolic register, turning instead to events and phenomena that defy the assumptive principles of common sense or reasoning. In some traditions, the spirit world has long been connected to political resistance: of the Haitian Revolution, C. L. R. James wrote that "voodoo [sic] was the medium of the conspiracy."[1]

This special issue considers the imponderable in relation to the normative: alien abduction, parallel worlds, visceral mysticism, possession by prion viruses, ghostly mediation, and more. The issue features the critical work of five authors, as well as three artistic interventions: poetry by Cristina Peri Rossi (translated from the Spanish by Liz Rose), as well as Oksana Vasyakina and Elena Kostyleva (translated from the Russian by Helena Kernan). Each contribution speaks to and across different valences of the paranormative, attending to forms of life that do not return to "the normal" but instead stage its undoing. As more and more of our shared present converges with the paranormal, we ask: To what extent can the "paranormative" resist capital and white supremacy, and to what extent is even the shifting ground of the normal open to commodification?

The first of our contributions, Jack W. Chen's "Poetry, Ghosts, Mediation," turns to classical Chinese ghost poetry—poems literally authored by ghosts—to reflect on the paranormative dimensions of lyric poetry as such. Building on and departing from contemporary media theory, Chen's account of ghost poetry as an analog "necrotechnology" through which the dead both speak and take "a kind of ghostly possession" of the mind and body of the reader gives us an alternative to influential positions on the nature of lyric poetry currently on offer, whether transcendental or historicist. What is interesting for Chen about classical Chinese ghost poetry has little to do with mimesis or representation; rather, the particular ontology of the ghost—one that has, in Chen's words, "no original substance . . . except that which is within the substrate that provides it with substance"—evinces a concept of mediation that helps us think about the nature of lyric poetry in general. Refining Jacques Derrida's notion of hauntology (*l'hantologie*), Chen argues that the ghost is only ever a mediated trace; that is, for the ghost the medium is quite literally the message—"it is only ever mediation." Much the same can be said for lyric more generally, as "what poetry communicates through the affordances of language is constituted by those affordances." That is, even when authorship is not attributed to ghosts, the nature of the lyric poem as such is isomorphic with that of the ghost: "the poem as the ghost in analog form, the mediation of the ghost as poetic speech, both uttered in the empty air and transcribed for the literary-historical archive."

Also looking to the literary as a site in which the normal is interrogated and destabilized, Delali Kumavie's contribution, "The Para-Worlds of Lesley Nneka Arimah's *What It Means When a Man Falls from the Sky*," advances a notion of the paranormal as "the distortion of the system" of ongoing and constitutive structural violence "that can be seen yet cannot be made real." Through close reading of Arimah's genre-defying 2017 short story collection and its interweaving of magical, animist, mythical, scientific, and realist modes, Kumavie draws out the paranormal as both a frame and a concept—*para* here is taken seriously as denoting the ancillary, rather than the oppositional, character of the concept under consideration—that renegotiates our relationship to the world-constituting violence emblematized by the events of 1492. In contrast to accounts that would seek out a post- or decolonial "third space" of hybrid or cosmopolitan subjecthood as a form of resistance, Kumavie leverages the paranormal to make visible the constitutive violence undergirding modern epistemological categories. Arimah's work, then, is not an example of magical realism, sci-fi, or speculative fiction, for such a designation would, for Kumavie, place her squarely within the same modern epistemological paradigm, characterized by "modernizing" imperial violence, on the one hand, and "originary" Indigenous culture, on the other. Rather, what Arimah's work offers is the revelation of "the parallel worlds on which the world is structured," which destabilizes the normal, "reveal [ing] the cracks in the world and its unease with Blackness."

Brandon S. Callender, like Kumavie, is interested in how to theorize Blackness vis-à-vis the paranormative. Callender's essay "The Devil Finds Use: Black Queers Do *The Exorcist*" operates against the reigning claim within Black horror studies today: that "normal" Black life is more horrific than the supernatural or, we might say, the paranormal. Callender traces this notion to James Baldwin's 1976 critique of *The Exorcist* in *The Devil Finds Work*, where Baldwin disidentifies with the paranormative horrors on offer in the film, instead turning to the systemic horrors of the normative world. Callender seeks to recuperate what might be lost in this dismissal of paranormative horror in favor of "yet another sobering encounter with the real" by reading three contemporary Black gay authors united by an "idiosyncratic and even playful [attachment]" to *The Exorcist*. Here Callender's interest is in how Larry Duplechan's *Eight Days a Week* (1985), James Earl Hardy's *B-Boy Blues* (1994), and G. Winston James's *Shaming the Devil* (2009) mobilize an aesthetics of possession to queer ends, troubling the boundaries between agency and passivity. Thinking with José Esteban Muñoz's notion of disidentification, Callender argues that Black and queer subjects can disruptively but productively locate themselves within the horror genre in ways that may have little to do with its intended reception. Sites of paranormativity—here of possession—become spaces for vexed, complex identification and disidentification, and sites of pleasure. Increasing the purview of Black horror studies to entail sites of the periphery of the normative ensures that we resist the naturalization of a single story of Black life as trauma, and the Black audience as obligated to confront that "singular collective trauma" in every experience of the genre. Multiple traumas, and multiple pleasures too, Callender reveals, can proliferate as they ramify across disidentifications with the camp of possessive aesthetics.

Pivoting away from the potentialities of literature and cinema, our final two contributions interrogate the paranormative dimensions of ontology, and indeed of nonrelation. Kathleen Powers's piece, "The Prion as Nature's Undead," turns directly to Georges Canguilhem's criterion for life, biological normativity, to examine the prion, a protein that infects the central nervous system and reproduces without the presence of DNA. The power of the prion and its associated, notoriously incurable diseases themselves appear ghostly: the prion cannot be destroyed by the body or regular sterilization precautions; it eludes modern pharmacology. Powers argues that Canguilhem's biological normativity is a spatial phenomenon that the prion defies, "perpetuat[ing] itself in a biology without language where the reproductive principle is not code but form." Rather, the prion "misfolds," producing the surrounding environment in its image. If Canguilhem imagines the organism "in *conversation* with its environment," a metaphor that evokes some dynamism, Powers offers a reading of how information exchange occurs for the prion unidirectionally along a fold—the environment, in this paranormative model, does not speak back to the prion. By attending to the peripheries of our norms of life—and, indeed, looking toward an eventual future in which those norms and gene-based philosophy of biology no longer hold—Powers offers a philosophy of biology that attends to the analysis of space and form rather than the traditional analysis of language.

Finally, Jonathan Jacob Moore's "Starships and Slave Ships: Black Ontology and the UFO Abduction Phenomenon" uses an Afro-pessimist grammar to understand the case of Barney Hill, the first and only popular Black alien abductee. For Moore, the absence of Black abductees in the many studies of the phenomenon is a question not of representation but of ontology. Following recent work in Black studies that "calls into question the popular assumption that Black life can *be*, unencumbered by the structural violence that initiated and conditions it," Moore posits a correspondence between the constitutively white experience of alien abduction and the hold, "the loud and breathing domain of the socially dead." Borrowing terminology from Frank B. Wilderson, Moore reads alien abduction as an example of "subjective vertigo"—in it "the unauthorized movement of the human *body*" may trouble the abductee's self-perception, but never their ontology. The latter—"objective vertigo," or "the structural violence that constitutes Black life before performative violence arrives on the scene in the form of badge, bad guy, or blue-skinned humanoid"—is something from which non-Black subjects are ontologically immune. Barney Hill fails to be a proper alien abductee, then, because "the alien abduction phenomenon is an experientially inaccessible domain for the Black nonsubject" and, moreover, because "this paranormal event" is in fact "a mundane quality, and the first condition, of Black life."

Is the experience of the paranormative, then, a site inaccessible to the Black nonsubject, as Moore would have it, or accessible only through disidentifications, following Callender? For Kumavie, the "para-world" of Arimah's short stories is what reveals the structures of violence of the normative world order, disrupting and contending with them. In this framework, the para-world is both the site of the Black nonsubject's exclusion and the place where the normative world's unease with Blackness is uncovered, made legible. Chen and Powers, meanwhile, both offer—in their disparate fields of literature and philosophy of biology—a conception of the paranormative as a kind of possession: for Chen, we can conceive of the classical Chinese ghost poem, as well as the lyric more broadly, as possessing the mind and body of the reader, while for Powers, the prion reproduces spatially by enfolding and compressing—we might say possessing—its environment. The paranormative in both these readings upends more typical positions through which to conceptualize the nature of lyric poetry or gene biology. Indeed, we might say that what unites these disparate pieces is their impulse to read paranormatively: cutting across identifications, and through variously encoded disciplinary ways of thinking and writing, each essay in this special issue interrogates our understandings of what is "normal." As life—biological and otherwise—recedes from such norms, these essays ask after what lies beside them.

Note

1. James, *Black Jacobins*, 86.

Reference

James, C. L. R. *The Black Jacobins: Toussaint L'Ouverture and the San Domingo Revolution*. 2nd ed. New York: Vintage, 1962.

Poetry, Ghosts, Mediation

JACK W. CHEN

In 718, at the beginning of a golden period in Tang dynasty China (608–907), there was a ghost who composed a poem. This poem was preserved along with its framing anecdote, which I translate as follows:

Ghost on the Riverbank 河湄鬼, "Poem of Embarrassed Thanks" 愧謝詩

In the sixth year of the Kaiyuan reign [713–41], there was a man who moored his boat on the banks of the Yellow River. He saw withered bones on the shore, so he tossed some food over. A moment later he heard, out of thin air, the sound of embarrassed thanks and was also presented with this poem.

開元六年。有人泊舟于河湄者。見岸邊枯骨,因投食而
與之。俄聞空中愧謝,幷贈此詩。

I was originally a scholar from Handan,　　　　我本邯鄲士。
On official business, I died by the riverbank.　　祇役死河湄。

QUI PARLE　Vol. 31, No. 1, June 2022
DOI 10.1215/10418385-9669459　© 2022 Editorial Board, *Qui Parle*

> Unable to have my family weep for me, 　不得家人哭。
> I've troubled you, a passerby, to mourn. 　勞君行路悲。[1]

Ghosts appear so often in premodern Chinese textual sources that it is commonplace among scholars to remark on the frequency of ghostly manifestations in literary, religious, historical, and philosophical writings. On this point, Robert F. Campany quotes the eminent scholar Arthur Waley: "There seem to be more ghost-stories in China than in any other part of the world; which is not unnatural, for more people have lived and *died* in China during more centuries than anywhere else."[2] One might say the same thing for ghost poetry in China. In fact, this poem is one of about a hundred poems attributed to ghosts during the Tang dynasty and collected in the *Quan Tang shi* 全唐詩 (*Complete Tang Poems*), a vast anthology of (almost all) extant Tang poems compiled during the Qing dynasty (1644–1912).[3] Many of these ghost poems have short occasional frames. Some were once embedded in longer pseudohistorical narratives, and others have no surviving contexts. There were a number of earlier ghost poems, and many more are from later periods; taken together, this corpus of poems by restless spirits comprise a significant minor tradition in the history of classical Chinese verse.

The poem itself is a simple composition, a polite message of interest mainly because it issues from beyond the grave. The ghost first informs the traveler that it was formerly a traveling official who happened to meet his end on the riverbank, far from home. It is both embarrassed and grateful (*kuixie* 愧謝) to the traveler for the gift of food, a spontaneous and perhaps facetious act of generosity that is taken by the ghost as a sacrificial offering. Yet in this awkward feeling of gratitude we see the ghost's sorry condition, how it cannot enjoy such offerings from its descendants, having been forgotten on this riverbank far from home. As Mu-chou Poo wrote, "When a ghost receives burial and sacrifice, he becomes the ancestor of his descendants, although still a ghost to others."[4] Here the possibility of ancestorship is foreclosed, condemning the dead spirit to the neglect of ghosthood. Ghost stories—and ghost poems—are thus always about "other people's ancestors," as Campany has put it, and "not their own."[5] Indeed, that ghosts are dispossessed others may be considered the very condition of ghostly possession.

Even if we never learn its name, the ghost is stirred to speech precisely because the traveler acknowledges that the desiccated bones are more than just things, that they were once the physical substrate for personhood—the medium through which personhood is realized. The poem is thus both a response to the traveler whose action confers personhood on what had fallen into thinghood and the very mediation of the ghost. Related to this is how the ghost and the traveler may be seen as doubles displaced in time, one arriving belatedly at the same place where the other once was. This poem—and a number of others in the corpus of surviving ghost poems—may be read as illustrating the theme of memento mori, in which an encounter with the dead is meant to remind the living person that he (invariably a male except in fictional narratives, where female ghosts predominate) will one day also die, a reminder that may also extend to the reader of the poem.[6] Although the classical Chinese tradition does not name this theme as such, it is commonplace in encounters with the returned dead. Here the ghostly spirit demonstrates just how vulnerable and contingent are the memory of names, the power of social rank, and the love of one's family once one has departed this earth. Travelers who jestingly acknowledge the bones of the ghost may one day find themselves in the ghost's place, hopeful that someone else will come along and restore them to some semblance of personhood.

It should be acknowledged that the very existence of ghost poetry in the Chinese literary tradition is surprising. As far as I can ascertain, no other literary tradition, premodern or modern, has treated ghosts as authors in their own right. That is, when ghosts compose poems in other literary traditions, they do so as acts of impersonation, in the voices of the dead, but not by the dead themselves.[7] By contrast, in the classical Chinese archive, ghost poems are not composed *as if* by ghosts but are understood to have been *actually* composed by ghosts. At the same time, anthologies that included ghost poetry did not treat ghostly authors exactly as they did historical male poets of public standing and reputation, which comprised the norm for the concept of authorship. Anthologies typically isolated the heterodox from the orthodoxy of male elite poets, sometimes devoting the entirety of the collection to a single strange or unusual category. As an example of this, there is a famous anthology devoted only to ghosts: the late Ming dynasty (1368–1644) *Caigui ji* 才鬼記 (*Record of Talented Ghosts*), compiled by Mei Dingzuo 梅鼎祚 (1549–1615).[8] For comprehensive anthologies, however, the category of ghost would have to be separated from normative poetic categories. Thus the aforementioned *Quan Tang shi* devised an elaborate system of categories for its marginal authors, beginning with dynastic traitors and rebels and ending with poems that could not be attributed to known authors. In the middle of these were poems by women, Buddhist monks, Daoist priests, male and female immortals, divine spirits, ghosts, and anomalies (such as talking animals). In this way, it was possible both for authorship to be attributed to ghosts and for the heterodoxy of ghostly authors to be acknowledged.

This brings us to the broader question of why this ghost, and other ghosts in medieval China, should have composed poetry in the first place. In histories of ghosts across the world's cultural archives and imaginaries, we find various forms of haunting between the dead and the living, from the displacement of material objects to apparitional manifestation, from disembodied voices and knockings to unexplained cold spots. These are all forms of communication if we define communication in the broad sense of a transfer of information (in whatever form information takes) between two minds (actual or virtual).[9] Yet poetry, which is almost universally evidenced across the world—not unlike ghosts—is almost entirely absent from histories of ghostly communication. To be sure, poetry is not usually understood in terms of communication in the first place, as the poem, transcending mere semantic exchange, cannot simply be reduced to its message and remain poetry. Recall here Cleanth Brooks and "the heresy of paraphrase," in which he argues that "what the poem *really* says" cannot be captured as "a summarizing proposition," that is, translated into "a rational statement."[10]

Yet the poem exceeds whatever logical message it might convey not only because of metaphorical or figural complexity, as the New Critics would have it, but also because of the poem's material medium, its mediation through language. This is what Paul Valéry intuited when he wrote the aphorism "Le poème—cette hesitation prolongée entre le son et le sens" (The poem—this prolonged hesitation between sound and meaning). Roman Jakobson, following Valéry, argued that poetry "is a province where the internal nexus between sound and meaning changes from latent to patent and manifests itself most palpably and intensely."[11] The materiality of poetic language, or indeed the materiality of language itself, is evidenced in the negotiation between the acoustic and the semantic aspects of the sign, between the sign's physical presence and its position within the differential system that produces meaning.[12] What poetry communicates through the affordances of language is constituted by those affordances, whether metaphor or sound; these material and rhetorical capacities mediate poetry's informatic processes, determining what may be communicated and how communication takes place.

Elsewhere I have argued more generally for poems and poetic divisions as mediating forms of informatic management and exchange in China, but here I want to focus on the idea of communication in poetry and consider how ghost poetry, like other forms of haunting, thematizes communication.[13] In this way, I am asking what it is about ghosts in China, or about poetry in China, that affords haunted communication through poetic form, and what this question might tell us about the nature of ghosts and of poetry more generally. Here, following the work of John Guillory, I shift the usual grounds of literary inquiry from representation to mediation. Like Guillory, I see a theoretical blind spot occasioned by the absence of the media concept, but whereas Guillory's project is to delineate the history of how "the concept of a medium of communication was absent but *wanted* for the several centuries prior to its appearance," I will read the concept of media into medieval Chinese ghost poetry, showing how the communicative dimensions of ghosts and poetry both enact, and are implicated in, processes of mediation.[14]

In many ways, the literary phenomenon of ghost poetry in classical China follows directly from how poetry is theorized in the tradition. The ghost is not represented in the poem that it bequeaths to the traveler but is mediated by the poem, translated analogically from one state into another, from spirit to voice to poem. As opposed to the privileging of representation over mediation in Western literary thought, the classical formulation of poetry in China can be read as emphasizing a medial conception that understands the poem as a communicative form.[15] This can be seen in the canonical understanding of poetry as it is first recorded in a late Warring States Period (475–221 BCE) text known as the "Canon of Yao" ("Yaodian" 堯典), a text collected in *The Esteemed Documents* (*Shangshu* 尚書), which in turn is one of the Thirteen Confucian Classics (*Shisanjing* 十三經). In describing this statement as canonical, I mean that it carries the full sanction of the classical tradition as formed through Confucian ideology and the imperial educational curriculum. Stephen Owen has translated the statement thus: "The Poem (*shi*) articulates what is on the mind intently (*zhi*); song makes language (*yan*) last long."[16] That is, the poem exteriorizes what is interior, a spoken communication of mind (the same word, *yan*, is used for "articulates" and for "language") that takes place through the materiality of poetic language. To put it another way, the poem is not only mind embodied but also mind extended into the world as a communicable object. The language of mimesis is not found in this conception of poetry; what we find instead is the translation of mind into poetic language, a medial conversion from one state of being into another. Further, the speaking of mind as poetry is prolonged as poetic song, which allows poetic speech to be extended not just in the moment but also implicitly across time as a song, which Owen notes has the capacity "to be preserved, carried afar, and transmitted."[17] Thus mind is extended beyond the private space of the self through poetic language, and language is extended across time through song. Indeed, it might be said that if poetry is the mediation of mind, then song is the mediation of poetry.[18]

The medial nature of poetry is further emphasized and elaborated in the Mao "Great Preface to the *Classic of Poetry*" (*Mao Shi daxu* 毛詩大序), a Han dynasty commentary attached to the first poem of the *Classic of Poetry*. This excerpt reformulates the earlier "Canon of Yao" statement. Again, in Owen's translation:

The poem is that to which what is intently on the mind (*zhi*) goes. In the mind (*xin*) it is "being intent" (*zhi*); coming out in language (*yan*), it is a poem. The affections (*qing*) are stirred within and take on form (*xing*) in words (*yan*). If words alone are inadequate, we speak them out in sighs. If sighing is inadequate, we sing them. If singing them is inadequate, unconsciously our hands dance them and our feet tap them.[19]

As Owen notes, the "Great Preface" revises the definition of poetry, focusing on the poem as the object produced by the mind's intent state rather than as what the poem enacts in articulating the intent mind. Owen then notes how this formulation "becomes the ground of the psychology of poetic theory and links the movement in the production of the poem to the 'extensive' aspect of communication" in the poem.[20] Indeed, this passage, even more than the "Canon of Yao" statement, emphasizes the communicative impetus that gives rise to poetry, describing not only how the mental state of intention is transposed into poetic language but also how the need to convey this interior state is supplemented by involuntary sighing, singing, and dancing when language is not sufficient. Of course the body, just as much as the poem, is a vehicle for the poet's mental state, a material channel through which mind may be communicated to the world.

Yet just as language affords a particular set of material capacities (and poetic language a set of linguistic constraints), so do the voice and the body. The "Great Preface" does not explain how the message of the poem changes as it moves from *zhi* to poem, from sigh to song, and finally to dance. These are analog mediations, but like all such mediations, the message is negotiated through the materiality of the media. In other words, the material affordances determine the possibilities of communication. The poem inflects *zhi* in one manner, channeling it through the strange constraints of syllabic count, rhyme, tonal balance, and parallel phrasing. The body channels the *zhi* in quite another, as it is possessed by a mental intensity so forceful that it impels dance—a possession that strongly recalls spiritual mediumship because the body seems to act at the behest of a mental command that is not quite the body's own. How can one say that the *zhi* is the same across these serial mediations, as if it were pure information or transcendent thought? Yet the "Great Preface" presents these mediations as a continuum or a logical progression, without attending to the transformations of expression and meaning that are entailed by the medial materialities, as if the medium fell away or were of no significance to the communicated *zhi*.

The forgetting of medium is, of course, a central argument made in media theory: we conveniently forget the means by which we apprehend the world, focusing only on the content, the *what* that is represented and not the *how*. This is Marshall McLuhan's example of the electric light bulb: "pure information" that is only ever the content of another medium as it is repurposed—remediated—by advertisements, television, and computer screens, and the like.[21] That is, we see not the light as such but what the light represents to us, and as the light is remediated, it further disappears into representation, so that all we ever see is the content of the medium, never the mediation. Jay David Bolter and Richard Grusin have characterized this disappearance of mediation as the "logic of transparent immediacy": the strategy for certain media forms to disappear and thus create the illusion of immediate (that is, unmediated) presence.[22] Yet this is not just a strategy of (post)modern media, a fall into simulation and simulacra that becomes more real than reality itself. Media have always traded on the claim to immediacy and presence, erasing their own material conditions and contexts.

To this end, both the poem and the ghost make claims of immediacy, whether as the seemingly direct presentation of private thoughts and feelings or the impossible manifestation of voice or vision, even as both the poem and the ghost are enactments of mediation, taking shape as media forms or even technologies, in the broadest sense of that term. If the poem claims to mediate thought or mind, ghosts haunt us through their capacity for mediation, the manifestation of their presence through the various forms of physical and nonphysical substrates. In the poem above, the ghost is anchored to the site of haunting by its bones, but then it translates into voice, and then into poetry, each of which provides a mediating substrate for its presence. These ghostly mediations are analog in nature—and may even be understood as analog signals, that is, temporally continuous (as opposed to discrete) transmissions of information within a given medium that use properties of the medium to convey the information. Whatever value is conveyed is proportionally analogous to a physical change exhibited by the medium: consider the way a glass thermometer measures heat by the expansion of the mercury in the hollow stem. In Brian Massumi's words, it is "a continuously variable impulse or momentum that can cross from one qualitatively different medium into another. . . . Like electricity into sound waves. Or heat into pain. Or light waves into vision. Or vision into imagination. Or noise in the ear into music in the heart. *Or outside coming in.*"[23] Ghosts are analog insofar as they are transmitted continuously in time across qualitatively different media—again, through the material and immaterial substrates that afford presence and presentation, whether these are architectural structures, human bodies, material objects, or dreams and visions.

At the same time, there is a question here of what, precisely, is the substance of the ghost that is transmitted in the first place, because unlike Massumi's examples of electricity or heat, the ghost is not energy and, in most cases, clearly not matter.[24] Indeed, the ghost resembles information, which Norbert Wiener has defined tautologically as a third term: "Information is information, not matter or energy."[25] Yet if the ghost is not energy, energy is nonetheless often used as a way of explaining ghosts. Contemporary popular belief has proposed that ghosts are composed of electromagnetic energy and can thus be detected by devices that measure electromagnetic fields.[26] Even here we find the work of the analog or, rather, of analogy, as the idea itself of the ghost is mediated by the idea of energy and thus given conceptual reality. That is, the idea of the ghost itself relies on an apposite metaphor that is then made literal, embodying the ghost as electromagnetic field disturbances. Therefore, rather than say that the ghost is analogically mediated, one might say that it is only the ghost's ontology that exists as analog mediation. That is, there is no original substance to the ghost except that which is within the substrate that provides it with substance. So, whatever a ghost is, whatever spirit is, in any empirical or epistemological sense what we come to experience is only its mediation. To put it another way, the ghost is only ever a trace presence, returned to the world of the living through the media forms that provide it access.

On this point, the concept of hauntology (*l'hantologie*) that Jacques Derrida invoked in his later work and that recalls his earlier work on the trace, among other terms, is useful. The ontological state of haunting may be understood both as posing a question of temporal paradox *and* as denoting the half state or half presence bound up with mediation.[27] Derrida, writing on the figure of the specter (*das Gespenst, le spectre*), comes close to saying that it is a mediation of spirit or ghost (*das Geist, l'esprit*) in visible form: "The specter is a paradoxical incorporation, the becoming-body, a certain phenomenal and carnal form of the spirit"; it becomes "some 'thing' that remains difficult to name: neither soul nor body, and both one and the other." He recognizes that spirit and specter are not the same thing but that there is something they share, and this quality is not knowable, "if precisely it *is*, if it exists, if it responds to a name and corresponds to an essence." What passes between spirit and specter is "this non-object, this non-present present," "an unnameable or almost unnameable thing," "something, between something and someone, anyone or anything, some thing, 'this thing,' but this thing and not any other, this thing that looks at us, that concerns us, comes to defy semantics as much as ontology, psychoanalysis as much as philosophy."[28] If Derrida hedges, hesitates, and ultimately fails to describe the nature of the ghost, it is because the ghost is knowable only when it takes form in the analogic transfers of media, and not otherwise, as there is nothing to know. As trace, the ghost is only ever manifest in its hauntological state; it does not belong to the order of representation; it is only ever mediation.

Still, even when the ghost is but a mediated trace, it imposes itself on our attention, forcing a presence all the more intensified by the media technologies that multiply and extend the ghost's reach. The fascination with ghosts that is widespread among media theorists and historians is not coincidental, though there is a tendency in media theory and histories of media to treat the advent of electrical technologies as marking an epistemic break with how we understand mediation, the past, and our relationship to the dead. For example, Friedrich Kittler contrasts the vague and private imaginary space of the book with the precise and public communicable image of the photograph; likewise, for Jeffrey Sconce, the telegraph invented the possibility of ghostly telepresence, transforming the relationship of the body to space and allowing ontological being itself to be converted into electricity and transmitted across physical wires.[29] While the imaging forth of the ghost in photography shaped the cultural imagination of what the ghost was—the now-familiar translucent, hovering, disembodied apparition—just as the telegraph reinvented ghostly communication in the form of unseen tapping at séances, these technologies represent changes of scale rather than of ontology.[30] As Guillory has noted, "Every communication is in that sense a telecommunication," which to say that the premise and necessary condition of all communication is distance, so the poem affords the extension of human capacities just as much as the photograph or telegraph claim to do.[31]

The questions both of time and of temporal paradox—indeed, of augmented vision—that are exemplified by the photograph are central to the lyric poem, which preserves and elevates a moment of time (what Sharon Cameron has discussed as *kairos*) and makes communicable what would otherwise be hidden (interiority, the private self, mind).[32] Like the telegraph, the poem erases both ontological and physical distance, staging an immediacy that may speak across the divides of world and history, life and death. As an ancient technology and media form, the poem has long transformed—and continues to transform—how human beings experience time and space.[33] Yet neither of the two major current positions on the nature of lyric as staked out by Jonathan Culler and Virginia Jackson, respectively—that is, a transcendental ideal of lyric and a historicist-processual one—engages with the mediating nature or capacities of poetry.[34] I have already mentioned Guillory, who argues that the privileging of representation (mimesis) over media is an organizing concept in the history of literary thought, but let me qualify this by invoking Earl Miner, who argued explicitly against lyric as primarily a mimetic genre. For Miner, the poem does not represent the poet or the poet's experience or some mental state of the poet but is chiefly affective or expressive. In this way, Miner's conception of lyric brings us closer to a communicative model and thus to a view of the poem as nonrepresentational medium.[35]

On this point, we might ask what this poetry is that has the capacity to mediate between the living and the dead, and indeed to give

voice to the dead, who speak to the living through the poetic medium, who *become* poetry. The figure of the ghost is, after all, a figure that does not exist independently of its material mediations,
whether these are the physical site of death, words spoken in empty
air, or the poem that makes its way into the literary archive. Just as
thought cannot exist without a body (not just the human body but
"hardware," as Jean-François Lyotard has noted), so the ghost is
bound to matter; there has to be a physical substrate that allows
the ghost to be present in the world.[36] Yet the experience of haunting
is one that often takes the form of a radical presence, an overwhelming and uncanny imposition of the ghost on the consciousness of the
witness, holding the witness in the suspended present that is the hall-
mark of the lyric poem. *Radical presence* is the phrase Earl Miner
uses to describe the experience of lyric poetry, which constructs a fu-
sion of time and space in which subjective interiority may be dis-
closed to the witness as if without mediation.[37] The ghost and the
poem emerge from analogical processes of mediation that simultaneously and paradoxically invoke Bolter and Grusin's logic of transparent immediacy. Perhaps this is what is meant by hauntology,
what Tom Gunning describes as "the ontologically ambiguous status" of the phantom as it puts forth "its uncanny claim on our
awareness and sense of presence" while resisting our attempts "to
integrate into everyday space and time."[38]

    I want to return to the ghost poem with which I began this essay.
We may say that the ghost comes to presence only as it traverses different analog mediations, beginning with something like mind or
thought (the disembodied *zhi*), then materialized as the sound of
voice speaking the words of a poem, and finally transcribed as a
text that may be circulated beyond its occasional moment. However,
there is an additional wrinkle: it is actually only in the moment of the
poem that we come to know the ghost, and in this moment we ret-
roactively construct the causality that has led to the moment of the
ghost's presence. (The anecdotal frame actually tells us nothing
about the ghost itself, just the circumstances around which the
encounter takes place.) This is what we do with all poems, in a way,
taking them as fragmented artifacts of a richer, more complex world
and attempting as best we can to restore that richness and complexity

through our acts of reading. It is, in fact, the poem that is the ghost's presence, the medium that is the message. The poem tells us as much, if we understand the speaking pronoun as mediated self: "I was originally a scholar from Handan, / On official business, I died by the riverbank." That is, we may read the poem as representation, as the mimesis of the poet articulated as the poem's speaker, but we may also read the poem as the ghost in analog form, the mediation of the ghost as poetic speech, both uttered in the empty air and transcribed for the literary-historical archive. This is no longer just ghost poem: it is ghost as poem, an analogical mediation of the ghost through the materiality of the poem. Thus, when we read the ghost as poem, we summon the ghost back to presence, allowing the ghost to emerge from the media through which it has traveled to reach us.

The ghost as poem is an experience of haunting, but this haunting takes place every time any poem is read aloud or silently. That is, the kairotic present of the poem is repeated each time the poem is voiced by the reader, a type of possession that marks yet another mediation of the ghost, whose subjectivity is reenacted by the living person who encounters the poem. The speaking "I" of the ghost takes possession of us as readers, but this is how lyric poetry operates, a kind of ghostly possession that allows both living and dead poets to reanimate their voices and minds in our bodies. All poets are effectively ghost poets—or will one day be ghost poets—who send snapshots of their minds out into the world like wandering spirits. For the dead who speak through poetry, their pasts become present once again in the moment of their reading, a temporal repetition that is the condition of hauntology. In this way, literary history is a history of the returning dead, a history of how poets are haunted by their predecessors and how we readers are haunted in turn when we bring the dead back to life.

Kittler famously wrote that "the realm of the dead is as extensive as the storage and transmission capabilities of a given culture."[39] And we may recall Sconce's insight that technology gives rise to telepresence, to ontologies that no longer are bound to immediate space and time. Yet the poem, like these later electrical and electronic mediations, is a necrotechnology, perhaps even one of the earliest, both serving as a medium for the ghost's transmission and simultaneously effecting mediumship itself by allowing the ghost to take possession of our minds and bodies. As with all necrotechnologies, the work of the poem is inextricable from the work of memory, itself a recurring theme in ghost stories as the inescapable, always present moment of the past that haunts us. How we properly lay the dead to rest—how we resolve the radical presence (and present) of the ghost—is what should mark the end of the haunting, but there is often no way to adequately respond to the ghost. The ghost does not really address us, even when the ghost addresses us. The traveler may have accidentally honored the ghost's unmourned remains, but the poem will remain as long as it is transmitted, a haunting that returns anew each time the words are read. The ghost's address is to us, yet it also goes past us, to the readers who will come.

....

JACK W. CHEN is professor of Chinese literature at the University of Virginia. Most recently he is author of *Anecdote, Network, Gossip, Performance: Essays on the "Shishuo xinyu"* (2021) and coeditor of *Literary Information in China: A History* (2021).

Acknowledgments

I am grateful to Yvonne Lin and the members of the *Qui Parle* editorial board for their insightful suggestions and comments, which greatly improved the essay. Thanks also to the International Network for the Study of Lyric for inviting me to present a very early version of this material at its 2021 conference, where I learned much from my fellow panelists and from the audience.

Notes

1. *Quan Tang shi* 全唐詩 (*Complete Tang Poems*), 24:865.9778. The poem was earlier preserved in the Northern Song literary encyclopedia *Taiping guangji* 太平廣記 (*Broad Records of the Taiping Reign Era*), 7:330.2621, with the ambiguous title "Person on the Riverbank" 河湄人. *Taiping guangji* attributes the tale to the nonextant collection *Lingguai lu* 靈怪錄 (*Registers of the Numinous and Weird*), which is either a textual error for *Lingguai ji* 靈怪記 (*Records of the Numinous and Weird*),

compiled by Zhang Jian 張薦, or *Youguai lu* 幽怪錄 (*Registers of the Hidden and Weird*), compiled by Niu Sengru 牛僧孺.

2. Campany, "Ghosts Matter," 15. Campany is quoting Waley, "Some Chinese Ghosts," 56. See also Yu, "Rest, Rest, Perturbed Spirit!"; Poo, "Completion of an Ideal World"; Poo, "Concept of Ghost in Ancient Chinese Religion"; and Poo, *Rethinking Ghosts in World Religions*.

3. On the *Quan Tang shi*, see Kroll, "Ch'üan T'ang shih"; and Broadwell, Chen, and Shepard, "Reading the *Quan Tang Shi*."

4. Poo, "Concept of Ghost in Ancient Chinese Religion," 178.

5. Campany, "Ghosts Matter," 18.

6. This is a major topos in classical and medieval Western art and literature, where epitaphic inscriptions called passersby to be mindful of their own mortality, and the legend of the Three Living and the Three Dead was illustrated in painting (though possibly derived from Indian Buddhist sources). See Ariès, *Hour of Our Death*, 218–21; and Binski, *Medieval Death*, 134–38. See also see Mills-Court, *Poetry as Epitaph*.

7. For an example of poetic impersonations of the dead, see Hammond, "Friendly Ghosts."

8. See Mei, *Caigui ji* 才鬼記 (*Record of Talented Ghosts*).

9. On the complexities of the term *communication*, see Peters, *Speaking into the Air*, 1–31.

10. Brooks, "Heresy of Paraphrase," 205–6, 211.

11. See Valéry, "Rhumbs"; and Jakobson, "Linguistics and Poetics," 373. This line of argument has been developed by Agamben, *End of the Poem*, 109–15; and Blasing, *Lyric Poetry*, 27–31.

12. Jan Assmann writes, "Every sign has two aspects, the aspect of its function within a sign system, by which it can refer to a specific meaning, and the aspect of its physical manifestation, by which it can indicate this meaning," in "Ancient Egypt and the Materiality of the Sign," 17.

13. See Chen, "Lines, Couplets, Stanzas."

14. Guillory, "Genesis of the Media Concept," 321.

15. To be sure, this is not how classical Chinese poetics would have described it. If there was no media concept in pre-twentieth-century Western intellectual history, there was certainly no explicit notion of media or mediation in classical Chinese thought. I should say that I am not interested in arguments derived from historicist nominalism. A culture may make arguments that gain nominalist visibility only in later periods, but this does not mean that the culture lacked access to the questions or concerns that impelled such arguments.

16. Owen, *Readings in Chinese Literary Thought*, 26. Here and in the following quotation, I have silently changed the romanization from Wade-Giles to pinyin.

17. Owen, *Readings in Chinese Literary Thought*, 29.

18. The classical Chinese model of poetic mind differs from how mind has been discussed in Western poetry. Cf. Hallberg, *Lyric Powers*, 105–42; and Skillman, *Lyric in the Age of the Brain*.

19. Owen, *Readings in Chinese Literary Thought*, 40–41.

20. This difference is discussed in Owen, *Readings in Chinese Literary Thought*, 40–41 (quotation on 41).

21. McLuhan, *Understanding Media*, 8.

22. Bolter and Grusin, *Remediation*, 21–31.

23. Massumi, "On the Superiority of the Analog," 135. See also Haugeland, "Analog and Analog"; and the extensive discussion with useful appendixes in Wilden, "Analog and Digital Communication." For more recent discussions, see Galloway, "Golden Age of Analog"; and Galloway, *Laruelle*.

24. The substantiality of the ghost is complicated in the classical Chinese tradition, where ghosts are both represented as immaterial yet able to participate in activities like sexual intercourse and even bear live children.

25. In Wiener, *Cybernetics*, 132.

26. See Morton, *Ghosts*, 129–45.

27. Derrida introduces the term *hauntology* in *Specters of Marx*, 10–12. See also Fisher, "What Is Hauntology?"; Blanco and Peeren, *Spectralities Reader*; and Shaw, *Hauntology*.

28. Derrida, *Specters of Marx*, 6.

29. See Kittler, *Gramophone, Film, Typewriter*; and Sconce, *Haunted Media*.

30. This is, in many ways, the achievement of spirit photography. See Chéroux et al., *Perfect Medium*.

31. Guillory, "Genesis of the Media Concept," 334.

32. Cameron distinguishes between *kairos* (the significant moment) and *chronos* (ordinary time) in *Lyric Time*, 120–21.

33. The "primitive" capacities of poetry are discussed in the first chapter of Welsh, *Roots of Lyric*, 3–24. Welsh draws on Ezra Pound's discussion of the "three kinds of poetry" in Pound, "How to Read."

34. See Culler, *Theory of the Lyric*; and Jackson, *Dickinson's Misery*.

35. Miner, *Comparative Poetics*, 9, 82–87.

36. Lyotard, "Can Thought Go On without a Body?," 79. This translation is reprinted in Lyotard, *Inhuman*, 8–23.
37. Miner, *Comparative Poetics*, 87.
38. Gunning, "To Scan a Ghost," 100.
39. Kittler, *Gramophone, Film, Typewriter*, 13.

References

Agamben, Giorgio. *The End of the Poem: Studies in Poetics*, translated by Daniel Heller-Roazen. Stanford, CA: Stanford University Press, 1999.

Ariès, Philippe. *The Hour of Our Death*, translated by Helen Weaver. New York: Knopf, 1981.

Assmann, Jan. "Ancient Egypt and the Materiality of the Sign." In *Materialities of Communication*, edited by Hans Ulrich Gumbrecht and K. Ludwig Pfeiffer, translated by William Whobrey, 15–31. Stanford, CA: Stanford University Press, 1994.

Binski, Paul. *Medieval Death: Ritual and Representation*. Ithaca, NY: Cornell University Press, 1996.

Blanco, María del Pilar, and Esther Peeren, eds. *The Spectralities Reader: Ghosts and Haunting in Contemporary Cultural Theory*. London: Bloomsbury, 2013.

Blasing, Mutlu Konuk. *Lyric Poetry: The Pain and the Pleasure of Words*. Princeton, NJ: Princeton University Press, 2007.

Bolter, Jay David, and Richard Grusin. *Remediation: Understanding New Media*. Cambridge, MA: MIT Press, 1999.

Broadwell, Peter, Jack W. Chen, and David Shepard. "Reading the *Quan Tang Shi*: Literary History, Topic Modeling, Divergence Measures." *Digital Humanities Quarterly* 13, no. 4 (2019). www.digitalhumanities .org/dhq/vol/13/4/000434/000434.html.

Brooks, Cleanth. "The Heresy of Paraphrase." In *The Well-Wrought Urn: Studies in the Structure of Poetry*, 192–214. New York: Harcourt, Brace and World, 1947.

Cameron, Sharon. *Lyric Time: Dickinson and the Limits of Genre*. Baltimore: Johns Hopkins University Press, 1979.

Campany, Robert F. "Ghosts Matter: The Culture of Ghosts in Six Dynasties *Zhiguai*." *Chinese Literature: Essays, Articles, Reviews* 13 (1991): 15–34.

Chen, Jack W. "Lines, Couplets, Stanzas." In *Literary Information in China: A History*, edited by Jack W. Chen, Anatoly Detwyler, Xiao Liu, Christopher M. B. Nugent, and Bruce Rusk, 119–24. New York: Columbia University Press, 2021.

Chéroux, Clément, Andreas Fischer, Pierre Apraxine, Denis Canguilhem, and Sophie Schmit. *The Perfect Medium: Photography and the Occult*. New Haven, CT: Yale University Press, 2005.

Culler, Jonathan. *Theory of the Lyric*. Cambridge, MA: Harvard University Press, 2015.

Derrida, Jacques. *Specters of Marx: The State of the Debt, the Work of Mourning, and the New International*, translated by Peggy Kamuf. New York: Routledge, 1994.

Fisher, Mark. "What Is Hauntology?" *Film Quarterly* 66, no. 1 (2012): 16–24.

Galloway, Alexander. "Golden Age of Analog." December 15, 2021. cultureandcommunication.org/galloway.

Galloway, Alexander. *Laruelle: Against the Digital*. Minneapolis: University of Minnesota Press, 2014.

Guillory, John. "Genesis of the Media Concept." *Critical Inquiry* 36, no. 2 (2010): 321–62.

Gunning, Tom. "To Scan a Ghost: The Ontology of Mediated Vision." *Grey Room* 26, no. 000 (2007): 94–127.

Hallberg, Robert von. *Lyric Powers*. Chicago: University of Chicago Press, 2008.

Hammond, Jeffrey. "Friendly Ghosts: Celebrations of the Living Dead in Early New England." In *Spectral America: Phantoms and the National Imagination*, edited by Jeffrey Andrew Weinstock, 40–56. Madison: University of Wisconsin Press, 2004.

Haugeland, John. "Analog and Analog." *Philosophical Topics* 12, no. 1 (1981): 213–25.

Jackson, Virginia. *Dickinson's Misery: A Theory of Lyric Reading*. Princeton, NJ: Princeton University Press, 2005.

Jakobson, Roman. "Linguistics and Poetics." In *Style in Language*, edited by Thomas A. Sebeok, 350–77. Cambridge, MA: MIT Press, 1960.

Kittler, Friedrich. *Gramophone, Film, Typewriter*, translated by Geoffrey Winthrop-Young and Michael Wutz. Stanford, CA: Stanford University Press, 1999.

Kroll, Paul W. "Ch'üan T'ang shih." In vol. 1 of *The Indiana Companion to Traditional Chinese Literature*, edited by William H. Nienhauser, 364–65. Bloomington: Indiana University Press, 1986.

Lyotard, Jean-François. "Can Thought Go On without a Body?," translated by Bruce Boone and Lee Hildreth. *Discourse* 11, no. 1 (1988–89): 74–87.

Lyotard, Jean-François. *The Inhuman: Reflections on Time*, translated by Geoffrey Bennington and Rachel Bowlby. Stanford, CA: Stanford University Press, 1992.

Massumi, Brian. "On the Superiority of the Analog." In *Parables for the Virtual: Movement Affect Sensation*, 133–43. Durham, NC: Duke University Press, 2002.

McLuhan, Marshall. *Understanding Media: The Extensions of Man*. Cambridge, MA: MIT Press, 1994.

Mei Dingzuo 梅鼎祚, comp. *Caigui ji* 才鬼記. In *Siku quanshu cunmu congshu* 四庫全書存目叢書, edited by Siku quanshu cunmu congshu bianzuan weiyuanhui 四庫全書存目叢書編纂委員會. Vol. 249. Jinan: Qi Lu shushe, 1997.

Mills-Court, Karen. *Poetry as Epitaph: Representation and Poetic Language*. Baton Rouge: Louisiana State University Press, 1990.

Miner, Earl. *Comparative Poetics: An Intercultural Essay on Theories of Literature*. Princeton, NJ: Princeton University Press, 1990.

Morton, Lisa. *Ghosts: A Haunted History*. London: Reaktion, 2015.

Owen, Stephen. *Readings in Chinese Literary Thought*. Cambridge, MA: Harvard University, Council on East Asian Studies, 1992.

Peters, John Durham. *Speaking into the Air: A History of the Idea of Communication*. Chicago: University of Chicago Press, 1999.

Poo, Mu-Chou. "The Completion of an Ideal World: Human Ghosts in Early-Medieval China," *Asia Major*, 3rd ser., 10, nos. 1–2 (1997): 69–94.

Poo, Mu-Chou. "The Concept of Ghost in Ancient Chinese Religion." In vol. 1 of *Religion and Chinese Society*, edited by John Lagerwey, 173–92. Hong Kong: Chinese University Press, 2004.

Poo, Mu-chou, ed. *Rethinking Ghosts in World Religions*. Leiden: Brill, 2009.

Pound, Ezra. "How to Read." In *The Literary Essays of Ezra Pound*, edited by T. S. Eliot, 25–31. London: Faber and Faber, 1954.

Quan Tang shi 全唐詩. 25 vols. Beijing: Zhonghua shuju, 1985.

Sconce, Jeffrey. *Haunted Media: Electronic Presence from Telegraphy to Television*. Durham, NC: Duke University Press, 2000.

Shaw, Katy. *Hauntology: The Presence of the Past in Twenty-First Century English Literature*. London: Palgrave Macmillan, 2018.

Skillman, Nikki. *The Lyric in the Age of the Brain*. Cambridge, MA: Harvard University Press, 2016.

Taiping guangji 太平廣記, compiled by Li Fang 李昉 et al. 10 vols. Beijing: Zhonghua shuju, 1961.

Valéry, Paul. "Rhumbs." In *Tel Quel*, 79. Paris: Gallimard, 1944.

Waley, Arthur. "Some Chinese Ghosts." In *The Secret History of the Mongols and Other Pieces*, 56–66. London: Allen and Unwin, 1963.

Welsh, Andrew. *Roots of Lyric: Primitive Poetry and Modern Politics*. Princeton, NJ: Princeton University Press, 1978.

Wiener, Norbert. *Cybernetics; or, Control and Communication in the Animal and the Machine*. 2nd ed. Cambridge, MA: MIT Press, 1965.

Wilden, Anthony. "Analog and Digital Communication: On Negation, Signification, and Meaning." In *System and Structure: Essays in Communication and Exchange*, 155–201. 2nd ed. London: Tavistock, 1980.

Yu, Anthony C. "Rest, Rest, Perturbed Spirit! Ghosts in Traditional Chinese Fiction." *Harvard Journal of Asiatic Studies* 47, no. 2 (1987): 397–434.

Two Poems by Cristina Peri Rossi

TRANSLATED BY LIZ ROSE

Cristina Peri Rossi was born in Montevideo, Uruguay, but has lived in Barcelona since the early 1970s, when she went into political exile. The only woman associated with the Latin American Boom, Peri Rossi has continued writing despite political repression, tenuous immigration status, and linguistic discrimination. She has published nineteen books of poetry and earned many literary prizes, most recently the 2021 Premio Cervantes.

My translations focus on the theme of lesbian intimacy as it relates to queer concepts of home in exile. Peri Rossi's portrayal of exile is woven with eroticism, affection, and affect made manifest in corporeal experience. Yet her work highlights what is in excess of the corporeal, especially what is beyond normative body/spirit and human/animal distinctions.

While "Blanca" and "Fertilization" describe distinct orientations to the paranormal, both texts engage the reader in unraveling the coherence of the normal. "Blanca" was first published in *Descripción de un naufragio* (1975), a collection of poems using a shipwreck as an allegory for the rise of the Uruguayan dictatorship. Peri Rossi's engagement with the visceral mystical in this poem is decidedly

QUI PARLE   Vol. 31, No. 1, June 2022
DOI 10.1215/10418385-9669470   © 2022 Editorial Board, *Qui Parle*

situated within the context of exile and transatlantic crossing. The poem highlights the disorientation of trauma and uprootedness and expresses a sense of being outside oneself, of watching the shipwrecked figure from without, and points to the psychic and spiritual impact of exile beyond the material realm.

"Fertilization" takes up the visceral mystical in a very different way. First published in her most recent collection, *Las replicantes* (2016), the poem fractures the concept of human fertilization by employing monstrosity, emphatically focusing on queer intimacy and parthenogenesis. The act of fertilization here centers language, hymns, gesture, memory, and ritual, rather than what can be physically incorporated into the body. Moreover, the poem likens this abnormal intimacy to the Christian conception of paradise. This blasphemous use of Christian mythology to narrate lesbian intimacy echoes Peri Rossi's early work, which was banned by the dictatorship in the 1970s. Through both poems Peri Rossi participates in a transnational tradition of lesbian feminist knowledge production that highlights the potentiality of queer intimacy and erotic power and ultimately argues for forms of relation that move against and beyond white heteropatriachy and reproductive futurity.

Blanca

White.
       Whether foam,
           or dove.
Forever laid
                on a beach path
land of the spirits
where the sands join together
and wind trembles in trees.
Wind trembles and sands sing.

As if the calm of the world
dwelled in her body, on her skin.
To have her like this,
              silent,
              white,

motionless,
free of time
of meetings and cities.

Monda. Smooth and bald like a statue,
    hairless but for light pubic fuzz,
    like a breeze
    where lips get caught
    the wind the afternoon the heat and the cry
    —saltwater I sipped between her legs.

Impenetrable.

Tossed in the air,
    rising and falling down her body
        swaying her like a reed,
    unable to feel
    unable to sigh
    unable to turn or respond.
    Wet with rain
    pouring endlessly on skin
    opening her pores like passages
    —where the entire sea entered.

Foreign.
    Isolated from delightful vices
    of moonlit nights
    and disquieting vices of afternoons
    of lovers without clocks.
    Isolated from delightful vices
    of suspect nights
    that call her alone to the sea
    and tossed
    at the mercy of the waters
    at the mercy of seaweed
    and approaching fish
    stalking her.

Settled in her home
       like fire in the hearth
       like a silent ancestor
       who no longer visits,
like mother and daughter.
       And loved by me
       as if she alone were both
       the desired mother
       and the fervent daughter.

As if she alone were both
the mother I loved one summer night
whose daughter I loved a lifetime.

Sealed.
       A secret kept from me
       a jagged oyster
       that could wound my fingers
       my face hands voice
       my thoughts and dreams,
       closed like an urn.
       Like a crypt.

Sacred.
       An untouchable goddess
       whose altar I visit each day with offerings
       —pine branches, laurel flowers,
       the fruits of a bounteous tree,
       leaving behind
       a trail of empty homages.

Still,
       fixed in time
       like a statue,
       so calm she seems dead,
       alone,
       unyielding,
       resistant to every siege,
       indestructible,

indifferent to loving partners,
impossible,
incapable of extracting her from me,

and so alone that sometimes I pity her.

Blanca

Blanca.
　　Si espuma,
　　si paloma.
Echada desde siempre
　　　　　　　　en un acceso de la playa
región de los espíritus
donde se dan cita las arenas
y tiembla el viento entre los árboles.
Tiembla el viento y las arenas cantan.

Como si toda la calma del mundo
se hubiera alojado en su cuerpo, sobre su piel.
Para tenerla así,
　　　　　muda,
　　　　　blanca,
　　　　　estacionada,
　　　　　aliviada del tiempo
　　　　　de citas y de ciudades.

Monda. Lisa e imberbe como una estatua,
sin más vello que una leve pelusa en el pubis,
como una brisa,
donde quedan atrapados los labios
el viento la tarde el calor y el llanto
—Agua salada que bebí entre sus piernas—.

Impenetrable.
Sacudida por el aire
que sube y baja de su cuerpo
　como a un junco contoneándola,
sin que ella lo sienta,
sin que ella suspire,

sin que ella gira o responda.
Mojada por la lluvia
que goteó una y otra vez sobre su piel
abriéndole los poros como puertas
  —por donde toda mar entró—.

Ajena.
Aislada de los deliciosos vicios
de las noches de luna
y de los vicios inquietantes de los mediodías
de amantes sin reloj.
Aislada de los deliciosos vicios
de las noches suspectas
que la hallaron sola junto al mar
y echada
a expensas de las aguas,
a expensas de las algas
y de los peces que arribaban
acechándola.

Instalada en la casa
        como el fuego del hogar
        como un antepasado mudo
        que ya no viene a visitarnos,
como la madre y la hija.
        Y amada por mí
        como si ella solo fuera al mismo tiempo
        la madre deseada
        la hija ardiente.

Como si ella sola fuera al mismo tiempo
la madre que amé una noche de estío
cuya hija amé toda la vida.

Lacrada.
        Cerrada para mí como un secreto,
        como la ostra de filosos labios
        que me hiriera los dedos
        la cara las manos la voz

el pensamiento y los sueños,
cerrada como una urna.
Como una cripta.

Sagrada.

Inviolable como una diosa
a cuyo altar yo llevara ofrendas todos los días
—ramas de pinos, flores de laurel,
los frutos del árbol opimo,
la miel, la música, los versos—
dejando, detrás,
una hilera de homenajes vanos.

Inmóvil,

fija en el tiempo
como una estatua,
tan quieta que parece muerta,
sólida,
inquebrantable,
resistente a todos los asedios,
indestructible,
mira indiferente amarse a las parejas,
imposible,
incapaz de desalojarla de mí,

y tan sola, que a veces me da lástima.

Fertilization

I fertilized you, filled you with me
flooded your empty being
the vagina of your body
your uterus
I filled you with words and remembrances
meetings and memories
filled your hollows with my gestures
with my jest
and once you were fertilized
I fled

I retreated to rest
a sated beast
maw bloody
your belly, your memory and being
full
you mumble and murmur still
on sleepless nights
you will spawn a tiny monster
a being ravenous as you
I won't be there to feed you again
your diet will be pathetic
straw and barren bones
but you will keep the memories
of happiness and hymns
of words and rituals
an encrypted paradise
we inhabit like Eve and her ovum
parthenogenetic.

Fecundación

Te fecundé te llené de mi
inundé tu ser vació
como la vagina de tu cuerpo
como tu útero
te llené de palabras y de recuerdos
de citas y memorias
llené tu hueco con mis gestos
con mis gestas
y después de fecundarte
me fui
me retiré a descansar
como una bestia saciada
de fauces sangrientas
tu vientre tu memoria y tu ser
estaban llenos
mascullas murmuras todavía
en noches en vela

engendrarás un monstruo pequeñito
un ser tan hambriento
como tú
No estaré para volverte a alimentar
tu dieta será pobre
paja y huesos secos
pero guardarás memorias
de alegrías y de himnos
de palabras y de ritos
de un paraíso cifrado
que habitamos como Eva y su óvulo
partenogenético, Eva.

....

LIZ ROSE is a PhD student in comparative literature and literary theory at the University of Pennsylvania. Their work has appeared in *Cagibi*, *The Poetry Project*, and *Raspa Magazine*, among other publications.

Acknowledgments

I am grateful to Emily Wilson and to the participants of the 2019 Bread Loaf Translator's Conference for their insightful and detailed comments on an earlier version of "Blanca."

The Para-Worlds of Lesley Nneka Arimah's
What It Means When a Man Falls from the Sky

DELALI KUMAVIE

"A Terrifying Future" or an Introduction

Lesley Nneka Arimah's collection of short stories, *What It Means When a Man Falls from the Sky*, offers the frightening image of a man falling from the sky as a physical event that evidences the unraveling of normative rationality. By so doing, the collection destabilizes the "common sense" epistemologies of the norm by insisting on an/other imaginary plane of existence.[1] Published in 2017, the stories persistently occupy an ever-shifting precipice where they unfix binaries that delineate the rational from the irrational, the normal from the paranormal, our world from other worlds. In the collection, the world can turn in a second: a loving sister on a mission to rescue her sister's items from an abusive boyfriend can end up shot by that same boyfriend; a mother long dead can return alive and well; and a child lovingly and desperately woven out of hair can become a bloodthirsty monster whose ashes form the foundations of another child. *What It Means* is a vivid, unexpected, and terrifying collection that collapses the armor of the past/present binarism with

QUI PARLE Vol. 31, No. 1, June 2022
DOI 10.1215/10418385-9669481 © 2022 Editorial Board, *Qui Parle*

which the world comforts itself. In this world, which opens with a story paradoxically called "The Future Is Bright," about a future bearing untold and unimaginable grief, both the present and the future occupy a violent continuum that is simultaneously pregnant with possibility, whether catastrophic or otherwise. Every story in the collection imagines the limits of normative thinking by narrating worlds as spaces where every norm is a point of contention.

Arimah's collection slips through the cracks of genres. By this I mean that the collection cannot be easily classified as magical realism, science fiction, or speculative fiction. It is this unruliness that is described by one reviewer of the book as Arimah's "flirting with horror fiction . . . ghost stories, and . . . an arresting form of magical realism in sync with Shirley Jackson, George Saunders and Colson Whitehead."[2] Another reviewer, Carmen McCain, posits that the book "range[s] from kitchen-sink realism to the wildly speculative."[3] While the label of magical realism hovers around the descriptive language that the collection has garnered, there is much in the collection to destabilize any cavalier labels such as this. Nevertheless, the framing of magical realism is impossible to escape; it imposes a kind of permeable boundary around the collection. In interviews Arimah has stated that she is invested in creating her own myths.[4] When asked about the inspiration for her story "Who Will Greet You at Home," Arimah responds by asserting that the story is her own invented myth because she is "taken by the idea of creating new myth that speaks to our current world in the same way that old mythology spoke to the world in its creator's time."[5] I propose that we read Arimah's stories as invested in forming new linguistic and narrative structures, a mythology, through which the world might be reflected. The stories therefore have less in common with magical realism than with Arimah's own metagenre, which reveals the parallel worlds on which the world is structured. In the narrative worlds of *What It Means*, banal worlds transform into grotesque ones where the thing that lurks in the dark could be a child woven out of hair, or the failing equations of a universalizing mathematical formula. In other words, Arimah weaves narrative worlds where the magical and the grotesque reside alongside unflinching realism.

The para-worlds that Arimah's stories create are, in part, a result of her own experiences "living between two places, [and] two norms."[6] Born in the United Kingdom, Arimah grew up in Nigeria, the United States, and other parts of the world where her father worked. Her experiences living across various continents and countries inform her narrative worlds and her storytelling. Her stories have won the African Commonwealth Short Story Prize, and an O. Henry Award for "push[ing] beyond conventional realism to mythologies."[7] The twelve stories in *What It Means* construct various parallel worlds that exist alongside each other. In these worlds, the operations of science, technology, innovation, mysticism, animism, and magic are not bound by the colonial binarism that casts European and white epistemologies, cultures, and structures of power as rational or scientific, and those by Indigenous Africans as primitive, irrational, and traditional. These para-worlds are structured by the accrued meanings of *para* (via etymology) as parallel, ancillary, *and* blocking/barricading structures. This means that reading Arimah's stories through generic literary genres such as magical realism, for instance, neglects how the stories use narrative temporality and structure to reveal a fundamental shift in the norm.

Indeed, the proximity the collection engenders between animism, science, technology, and magical realism functions as critical avenues through which we might examine the collection. These avenues constitute elaborations to the normative structures of the world as we know it, or what I describe as animism and magic *as* science that simultaneously situates Arimah's narrative worlds within the "globalizing" norms of colonialism and exceeds them. This means that the collection's weaving together of familiar settings with mythical and magical narrative plots and temporalities does not bifurcate animism and magic from science but rather positions them as simultaneous and interwoven. It is this coconstitutive existence of animism, magic, myth, science, and technology that Harry Garuba describes as a "logic of animistic thought" that posits "other histories of modernity beyond the linear, teleological trajectories of the conventional historical narrative."[8] By crafting a nonuniversal and "temporally transcendent" relationship between animism, magic, science, and technology,

What It Means upends the fictions of binaries.[9] The collection destabilizes and disfigures the neat historicity of modernity by merging the
familiar aesthetics of modernity with mysticism. Through a process
of "continual re-enchantment of the world" the "'magical elements
of thought' are not displaced, but on the contrary, continually assim-
ilate new developments in science, technology, and the organization
of the world within a basically 'magical' worldview." These acts of
"re-enchantment," according to Garuba, are persistently unfolding
in a process where "the rational and scientific are appropriated
and transformed into the mystical and magical."[10]

I take Garuba's reciprocal appropriations of and transformations
between science and animism further by positing that myth, magic,
and animism constitute a science of their own. Garuba argues that
animist realism exceeds magical realism because the "representa-
tional and linguistic practices" that underwrite it extend beyond
African literature and into a conception of the world one encounters in Toni Morrison's *Beloved* and Wole Soyinka's *Interpreters*.[11]
Garuba's framing of animist realism as a "predominant cultural practice of according physical, often animate material aspect to . . . an ab-
stract idea" points to the role language plays in structuring epistemologies and worlds.[12] Frantz Fanon in *Black Skin, White Masks* states
that "to speak a language is to appropriate its world and culture."[13]
I read Fanon's position on language and appropriation as key to
understanding how language and its myths (in the Barthesian sense)
construct and constitute interpretive frameworks.[14] In his reading
of language, David Marriott shows how language and speech in
Fanon carries "an additional signified," which is attached to the
Black body that "enunciates it."[15] According to Marriott, "Fanon
shows that French carries a promise—of worldly well-being, of
honor, wealth, dignity, and health—that remains virtual by reason
of the very racism by which the *colonisé* invest in its image and vil-
ify those who fall short of its enunciation."[16] Later he asserts, "The
reality of language can be understood as a kind of whitening and
the sign is experienced as an elective elocution, or seen to evoke only
white pretense, as if in every sign there were a trace, a 'morphology,'
that gives the *colonisé*, as if by precious miracle, a white interlocution,
and a white reality from which its blackness is excluded." In this way

language "gets caught up in a game of appearances, masks, and concealments."[17] Similarly, the matrices of meaning that are signified by delineating a literary work as magical realism, animist, or mystic conceal its distancing from the normative imaginaries that are designated as science fiction, for instance. Appropriating Marriott's words, I posit that there is an "additional signified" that literature by Africans, and about Africa, bear and that enables their separateness to be foregrounded, and their imaginaries to be delegated as mystical, mythical, and so on, but never scientific, or technological. In other words, the language we use to analyze and describe literature by African writers conceals its own biases by fixing such literatures in particular discursive silos.[18] Thus one line of inquiry this essay engages with below is a critique of magical realism not for its position as a subcategory of animist realism, as Garuba argues, but for its bifurcation of scientific method and technological innovation from magic and animism.[19] To forward this critique, I complicate how magical realism obscures forms of technological innovation by forcing under its vast umbrella narrative worlds whose foundational logics are rooted in a non-Western worldview. I do this by examining how Arimah's story "Who Will Greet You at Home," when viewed through a scientific method of technological innovations emerging from Africa, imagines reproduction as a technical skill that unites magic, animism, and science.

Overall, what this essay seeks to do is renegotiate our relationship to African literary texts by reconstituting our relationship to the normative. By circumnavigating the current discourse where non-Western literary and cultural criticisms are always already framed through opposition, resistance, or refusal, I move the conversation toward a parallel, ancillary, or barricaded approach where we can consider the coconstitutive structures through which hierarchies might be reexamined. By arguing that the incorporation and transformation of the scientific into the mystical and magical constitute parallel structures in Arimah's collection, I am suggesting that there is in Arimah's narrative worlds coexistence between the mystical and the scientific. To do this, I turn to Clapperton Mavhunga's assertion that the "versions of science, technology, and innovation" that exist currently leave very little room (often none at all) for versions that did not emerge out of European epistemologies and practices.[20] Mahvunga and his interlocutors, in their collection *What Do Science, Technology, and Innovation Mean from Africa,* call for a reassessment of scientific methods and epistemologies that exceed the current Euro-centered definitions and methodologies. What Mahvunga offers, in terms of my reading of Arimah, is a mode of reading that wrests science and technology from its restricted temporality (the colonial period) and its privileged sites of practice (the laboratory). It inspires a line of questioning and analysis that straddles the often-repeated divide between magic, animism, and science. Throughout Arimah's collection, epistemologies and metaphysics are simultaneously scientific, mystical, and magical, and they exist alongside each other, weaving into each other. It is in this interweaving that the normative is shifted and distorted. Arimah's worlds reveal the illusory binary between the scientific and the mythical, conceiving of them instead as entwined with and existing in tandem with one another. It is this understanding that blurs the lines that separates Arimah's worlds from our own.

Central to the interplay between the scientific, the mystical, and the magical is the temporal entangling of the past, present, and future in *What It Means.* Arimah asks us to reinterrogate the possibilities that are often woven into the future in popular discourse, such as when people assert that there are "Black people in the future" as a counter to the violent past and present of Black life. Arimah's narrative worlds ask, with Jared Sexton, whether the "future promis[es] anything different or, rather, better," and responds in the negative.[21] Indeed, her response locates the future along a continuum where the past repeats itself. One way in which Arimah's narratives help us think through futurity as repetition is in the protagonist of "Second Chances," who is unable to say what needs to be said when his mother returns from the dead, and instead seeks a logical reason to explain what his mother's return from the dead means for him and his family. Arimah suggests that when presented with the opportunity to act differently or atone for the past, we are often unable to accomplish that task. We often imagine that the past can be remedied in the future, but as these stories consistently show, the past, present, and future are continuums in which we repeat, with a difference, the violence of an earlier time.

In what follows, I provide an overview of my understanding of the normative and the paranormal, mobilizing that framing to read the eponymous story of Arimah's collection, "What It Means When a Man Falls from the Sky" ("What It Means"). I view the normative as the world-constituting structures instantiated in 1492, which were the catalyst for transatlantic slavery, colonialism, and ongoing neo-colonial projects and the paranormal, as Arimah's parallel world through which the structure of the world is revealed and animated. In particular, I examine how Arimah's world imagines futures that function as a continuum to reveal the ever-present structures of domination. In the second part of the essay, I argue that "Who Will Greet You at Home" functions as a paranormal frame because it disrupts the common sense of magical realism. Drawing on the reframing of science and technology that calls into question the roots of scientific methods and technological innovations, I argue that interpreting stories such as "Who Will Greet You at Home" as magical realism obscures the stories' attention to technological innovation.

Shifting the Emphasis: The *Para* in the Paranormal

The prefix *para-* creates a sense that the resulting term is "analogous or parallel to, but separate from or going beyond, what is denoted by the root word."[22] It signifies phenomenal positionality (as in "beside") or relationship to the root word.[23] We might thus consider *para-* as a vestibule through which the root word must enter to create often aporetic layers of meaning.[24] In words like *parasol*, *paravent*, and *parapet*, *para-* denotes a defensive shelter, a protective barrier, or a wall.[25] Thus the term *paranormal* derives its meaning from the additional framing that the prefix introduces and from the other denotative meanings embedded in the prefix and the root word. *Para-*, in this context, extends the root word to denote something simultaneously parallel and ancillary to the root term as well as something that shields, blocks, or barricades it.[26] Thus the *para-* in *paranormal* could also connote something that stands in the way of or even intentionally blocks or barricades the norm.

As the *Oxford English Dictionary*'s contextual definitions of the prefix show, the root word becomes primary in the meaning of the word; it is that which creates signification. But the root word in the paranormal—the norm, normal, or normative—is often perceived as antithetical to many of the theoretical inheritances through which Arimah's work can be positioned. The norm often designates the logic and structures against which critical interrogative methods and approaches are harnessed. In their assessment of normativity in queer studies, Robyn Wiegman and Elizabeth A. Wilson argue that even though one cannot say that conceptions of norm and normativity are identical across queer studies, those conceptions have become a "negative force against which the field crafts its self-definition, contestations over the history and multiple (and conflicting) disciplinary meanings of norms and normativity have been largely obscured."[27] Further, Wiegman and Wilson assert that criticisms that stem from a "commitment to antinormativity" shape work on "transgender, disability, affect, ecology, race, war, surveillance, colonialism, (neo) liberalism, sovereignty, incarceration, and the posthuman" by generating a "distinct vocabulary" and "a rhetorical mode of argument that continues to bear the promise of the world-making significance."[28] If antinormativity affords an oppositional stance that creates a web of entwinement between several interrelated (yet distinct) disciplinary fields and critical thought, then the normative marks both a common ground and a stable referent. It is, in some sense, a kind of common language of critical discourse that marks the object or system or institution to which an opposition is expected. By collapsing various fields of study and critical thought into a single realm, Wiegman and Wilson fail to address the varying shape and form of the normative in each instantiation. In other words, the normative in postcolonial studies, for instance, where the colonial structure and its innovations constellate as the institution against which postcolonial studies must interrogate and animate, is distinct from the norm of queer studies, which is in the heteronormative and its "barely containable, ever mobile hetero-geneity."[29]

It is important to note, as Wiegman and Wilson do, that the normative is not a closed scape; it is at best a permeable one under whose umbrella discourses, positions, experiences, conditions, and so on can be admitted and excised. Wiegman and Wilson describe the norm as "systemic" and later, citing François Ewald, aver that the norm has "no outside": it "integrates anything which might attempt to go beyond it."[30] An illustration of this permeability of the norm is offered in Saidiya Hartman's *Scenes of Subjection*, where she describes the impulse to normalize the violence of slavery by "neutralizing" and "assimilating" the observation of slavery's violence into "the normal, the everyday, the bearable."[31] By depicting such encounters with the violence of slavery as "socially endurable," Hartman argues that the observer, in this case Abraham Lincoln, effectively reinterprets the scene "from one of despair to one of contentment and endurance."[32] While the norm figures in Hartman as interpretive labor that repeats a landscape of discursive and epistemological sleight of hand, it also hints that the norm is best understood as the structural foundations of the world whose logics can embrace the various persistently innovating systems and structures at whose core is violence.

As a way of reading Arimah, therefore, I propose a consideration of the paranormal as a kind of structural other that disrupts binaries by offering a parallel or ancillary structure that animates, reveals, blocks, and disfigures the norm. It is a simultaneity that reveals another realm without instantiating that realm, and where the simultaneity of science and magic, for instance, is made evident. Adom Getachew conceives of the normative as "a world-constituting force that violently inaugurated an unprecedented era of globality," positioning it primarily as a globalizing structure that reorders the world.[33] The norm is instituted to create and maintain a world where Indigenous people in Africa, the Americas, Asia, and elsewhere were subjected to genocide, territorial dispossession, the transatlantic slave trade, and its continuing forms of violent dispossession through, for example, racial capitalism and its neoliberal counterparts. These world-constituting events of 1492 and their attendant technologies produced "a kind of human," as Iman Zakiyyah Jackson argues, which is distinct from the humanity embodied by Europeans.[34] These technologies of bifurcating the Human Other from the White Human also instituted a binary that transformed the epistemological structures of the world. The year 1492 extended a dualistic system that separated the scientific and rational epistemologies of Europe from the irrational, supernatural, and nonscientific knowledge of the

Others. This dualism persists despite an ever-expanding body of criticism that resists, opposes, and dismantles its aura. It is present when the fantastical and speculative worlds of non-Euro-American writers are described as "magical realist" instead of as science fiction, or in the continuing neglect of certain kinds of literature that unsettle well-worn interpretation, disciplinary methods, and analytics.

If the norm is the epistemic and structural foundation on which our existing systems are balanced, then when this norm is placed under the valence of the prefix *para-*, it diverges into the parallel or ancillary or notes the existence of a barrier. The relationship of the paranormal to the normal is not one of refusal, resistance, or opposition. Rather, it is a renegotiation of the normative that instantiates discontinuities to existing norms. The reterritorializing that opens the eponymous story of the collection, "What It Means," reveals a colonial continuum by imagining a paranormal world that predicts the inevitable reterritorializing that a warming climate will engender. This continuum where the aftermath of ecological disaster will catalyze a renewal of colonial dispossession and death is set in a future that is reminiscent of predictions of the world's future by climate scientists. Yet in Arimah's version it is not the so-called global South whose territories are depleted and destroyed by the warming climate; instead, it is the North, specifically Europe and the United States, that suffers the consequences of ecological destruction even though according to current predictions it is the island nations and coastal countries that will first experience the worsening effects of a warming climate. Arimah's slightly askew world functions as a paranormal structure that makes visible the structures of power that undergird the world.

Set in the future, in the aftermath of an ecological cataclysm that reinstitutes the modalities of colonial occupation in Senegal and Nigeria, Arimah's story "What It Means" rehearses the history of transatlantic slavery and colonial occupation even as the story points to the unique contours of the coming colonialism. In the story, the United States, Europe, and Russia are flooded after a series of ecological disasters. The only livable spaces that remain are in the global South, so the Americans flee to Mexico, the British to Nigeria, and the French to Senegal. Just as the world is losing hope, a Chilean mathematician, Francisco Furcal, discovers an infinite formula that explains the universe and allows some mathematicians—including the protagonist, Nneoma—to extract grief from the human body. Furcal's formula, through experimentation, also leads to the discovery of the formula for human flight. At the beginning of the story, however, we learn that a man falls from the sky while testing the formula for flight, suggesting that Furcal's formula might be failing.

One of the major thematic concerns of "What It Means" is the reinstantiation of territorial colonialism, a new form of colonial occupation that relies on biological weaponry to eliminate those already living on the land. The story reimagines the deadly consequences of territorial power under which colonized people exist despite the fictions of political independence. These structures of power and domination were also at the core of the thematic concerns of early modern African writers. However, what has changed since the colonial structure and its afterlives described so poignantly by writers like Chinua Achebe, Ngũgĩ wa Thiong'o, and Ama Ata Aidoo is that in the world Arimah fashions, it is no longer possible to speak of postcolonial hauntologies, or remains, but rather of a coming imposition whose form will be determined by a looming ecological upheaval.[35] While the cataclysm of climate disasters creates situations that are unknown, "What It Means" suggests that these futures will nevertheless exist along a continuum of existing structures. In other words, while the form or catalyst of the violence is different, its target is the same: in this case, the elimination of Africans to make room for displaced Europeans. This new/old structure of colonial rule is described by Chilean poet Daniel Borzutzky as "continuums of violence, of fear, of shame, of language, of terror, of slaughter, of broken bodies, of pollution, torture, ethics and power."[36]

In imagining how a cataclysmic environmental disaster catalyzes the normative structures of the world to reassert themselves in the event of a geographic reordering, Arimah depicts the conditions under which Africans exist as a form of the paranormal that constantly reveals the world's normalized capacity for violence. Axelle Karera warns, "Nothing guarantees thus far that the world we could inherent [inherit], in the event of successful post-apocalyptic/post-Anthropocenean times, would *de facto* be non-racist."[37] Further, Karera asserts that the inability to wrestle with "disposable blackness" in the critical discourse of the post-Anthropocene and the continuing "silence on race" means that there is a potential to "reproduce anti-Black sentiments."[38] What Karera's work theorizes, Arimah's narrative creates. In the fictional world of "What It Means," the ecological disaster reproduces the anti-Black structures that render the people across the African continent disposable.

In what the story describes as the "Elimination"—the development of biological weapons that target the melanin in Black skin—the story yields what Fanon calls "the epidermal racial schema" as the target of the new genocidal project.[39] The narrator of the story explains that the French, on resettling in "relative peace" in Senegal, develop biological weapons that target the melanin in Black skin to murder and claim Senegal for themselves. The narrator recounts: "The Elimination began after a moment of relative peace, after the French had won the trust if their hosts. The Senegalese newspapers that issued warnings were dismissed as conspiracy rags, rabble-rousers inventing trouble. But then came the camps, the raids, and the mysterious illness that wiped out millions. Then the cabinet ministers were murdered in their beds."[40] In places like Nigeria, renamed Biafra after the Biafran Independence War of the late 2030s, the British had sought help and been granted access to live. Later, these same British would "demand their own separate government" by threatening to "deploy biological weapons"; this would lead to the formation of the "Biafra-Britannia Alliance," in which Nigeria's land, government, and grievances are shared between the British and the Nigerians.[41] While this arrangement guarantees citizenship for Indigenous Biafrans, many, as the story narrates, become "third class citizens" who work in the service economy to serve the British. As third-class citizens, these Biafrans must use Anglicized names because "the Britons preferred their service workers with names they could pronounce, and most companies obliged them."[42] These arrangements, which on the surface seem to be political arrangements with social and economic effects, are in fact totalizing, because they fundamentally restructure and rearrange the Biafran nation-state. Under this new arrangement, Biafrans are forced to live in the periphery serving as a "servant" class for the British. Earlier colonial projects in West Africa were founded on a logic of extraction that relied on the people who occupied these colonized territories as a resource that facilitated extraction and allowed the ruling nation to expend minimal resources to sustain this extraction. While at its root the colonial project in Africa, like transatlantic slavery, was founded on a logic of "disposable blackness" (to use Karera's term), the form of disposability we find in "What It Means" does not mask the killing of Africans as a "civilizing mission," but sidesteps the discursive justification for outright elimination. Thus what Frank Wilderson describes as the process that "reconfigures the African body into Black flesh"[43] is overstepped because the history that Arimah rehearses supplements and allows the inhabitants in Senegal and Nigeria to be eradicated to reestablish the order that situates Europeans as the leaders of the world once again.

While the ecological disaster and the subsequent elimination of Africans for their territories constitute a central thematic concern of the story, it is the mathematical formula discovered in the aftermath of these disasters that serves as the conceptual framework. By this I mean that the mathematical formula, which provides the possibility of a continued human existence in the story, is also the means of its unraveling. When Furcal's formula is discovered, Neoma tells us, it is believed to have "no end and, perhaps, by extension, [that] humanity [too] had no end."[44] The formula replaced the void created following the reorganizing of the geography of the world as the climate disasters made North America and Europe unlivable. After extensive testing and experimentation, the formula allowed for the discovery of equations that "coincided with the anatomy of the human body," making it possible for Nneoma and others like her to remove memories and grief from the human psyche and body. Yet, as Nneoma explains, the formula has limits: it is impossible to work on people who are close to you, as exemplified by Nneoma's failure to excise his father's grief after the death of her mother. Nevertheless, there are supercomputers dedicated to testing the formula's "infiniteness."[45] Indeed, after the highly publicized fall of a man who was testing the equation for flight derived from Furcal's formula, rumors of the failure of the formula lead Nneoma to reassess her role as someone who removes grief from people using the same formula. As the mathematical formula begins to unravel in "What It Means," so too do the things that are enabled by its existence, such as the ability to extract grief and the ability to defy gravity and fly. This mathematical formula, in essence, provides the means to edit our memories and emotions, and the physical and biological limits of our bodies. While the formula allowed for the institutionalization of a new era of the normative, its reconstitution of the biological and physical laws proves unable to sustain its own logic.

If we view Furcal's formula as a mathematical rationality that, according to Calvin Warren, functions as "an assemblage of practices, operations, and procedures designed to *formalize* knowledge, ethics, value, ontology, and philosophies of life and death," then the unraveling of the formula can also be explained. Warren asserts that "mathematics is the *formalization of thinking itself.*" It *is* "thinking."[46] Warren situates a tension between the form and antiform, between mathematics that attempts to "preserve black life," per Katherine McKittrick, and one that "offers the destruction of mathematical form to arrive at plenum, pure matter," per Denis da Silva, as two modes through which mathematics can be used to theorize Blackness.[47] However, the mathematical tensions in "What It Means" are less about the formulation of Blackness through mathematics' relationship with economics, and more about how the logics of technology and science, while permitting innovations, also create the conditions that yield Black people globally to the enduring violence that structures the world.

In Arimah's narrative world, the unraveling of Furcal's formula mirrors the unraveling psyche of those on whom it conferred the ability to edit human anatomy and emotions. At the end of the story, when Nneoma's former girlfriend, Kioni, who extracts grief from "displaced Senegalese and Algerians and Burkinababes," arrives at Nneoma's home with "scratches and bites concentrated below the elbow," suggestive of autophagia, we are primed to understand that this is ultimately evidence of the unraveling formula. Nneoma, faced with Kioni's inevitable demise, thinks:

> How many people had Kioni worked with over the last decade?
> Five thousand? Ten? Ten thousand traumas in her psyche, squeezing past each other, vying for the attention of their host. What

would happen if you couldn't forget, if every emotion from every person whose grief you'd eaten came back? It could happen, if something went wrong with the formula millions and millions of permutations down the line. A thousand falling men landing on you. Nneoma tried to retreat, to close her eyes and unsee, but she couldn't. Instinct took over and she raced to calculate it all. The breadth of it was so vast. Too vast.[48]

Here Nneoma provides the clearest articulation of the unending trauma that those who survive the violent territorial dispossession endure, and the effect of that grief on those who work to remove it. Indeed, Nneoma attempts to put a numerical figure to the grief and trauma that Kioni has "eaten," and by so doing we understand that she is continuing to work with the mathematical logic in which she is trained. As mathematicians who remove grief, Kioni and Neoma essentially consume the grief of others and incorporate that grief into their own beings. As Neoma begins to grasp the infinitude of the problem, she returns to the image that begins the story, but this time attempting to give its true innumerable scope, "a thousand men falling landing on you."[49] The paranormal in "What It Means" reveals the conceptual interplay between the past of Blackness with its imagined future as a continuum, one in which the violence of the past reproduces itself in the present and future. In this para-world the future functions as an indexical space where the past and present can be dissected. In Arimah's worlds, the future reveals the continuums of violent structures that actualize the impossibility of freedom.

Beyond Magical Realism: The *Paranormal* and the Parallels of Animism

Magical realism, as an increasingly inadequate interpretative lens, continues to linger in the critique of writers whose narratives create worlds deemed "alternate" or "other" to the realist worlds of modernity. According to Brenda Cooper, "Magical realist writers have an urge to demonstrate, capture and celebrate ways of being and of seeing that are uncontaminated by European domination. But at the same time, such authors are inevitably a hybrid mixture, of which European culture is a fundamental part."[50] That writers of "magical realism" are themselves influenced by the European worldview that their works seek to destabilize might signal a slippage in the interpretative move that attributes Indigenous cosmovision to writers who themselves have been trained in European institutions, or who no longer live in the communities whose alternative approach to the world their narratives supposedly capture. However, these writers, according to Copper, exist in the "fertile interstices" that "[capture] the paradox of the unity of opposites" while also contesting "polarities."[51]

Later Cooper describes magical realism as "syncretizing uneven and contradictory forces" through plot. She explains that ideals of utopia are "recurrent in magical realist dreams . . . [and] stand for the possibility that such unity might ultimately be achieved in societies where this currently appears only as a slight hope." Cooper asserts that the societies represented in magical realist fiction in West Africa are "in transition, uneven, the product of different cultures, stages of economic development and undergoing transformation. The function of the magical realist plot is to represent history by symbolizing these mixtures as meaningful."[52] While Cooper continues by saying that the genesis of this interplay between history and Indigenous beliefs permit "simultaneous modernizing and . . . returning to an original, nurturing source," there remains a tension that characterizes Indigenous ways of being as "original" and "nurturing" while the world instantiated by transatlantic slavery, colonialism, and ongoing forms of imperialism are read as "modernizing." My critique of magical realism emerges from this very interplay between the "mysterious, sensuous, unknown and unknowable" in what is called magical realism and "the fictional space [of] history."[53] Cooper's arrival at magical realism is woven through a detailed analysis of the key textual debates of postcolonial studies: debates about colonial intellectuals and the hybrid postcolonial subject whose encounter with the metropole and cosmopolitanism results in the possibility of a hybrid "third space" where the magical can exist in tandem with the modern. Cooper locates the works of the writers she examines—Ben Okri, Kojo Laing, and Sly Cheney-Coker—as "suspended between Bhabha's cosmopolitan celebration of border traffic, on the one hand, and Soyinka's or Achebe's decolonizing boundaries, as national fortification on the other."[54] While the framework of Cooper's "third space," which at first glance might have potential for the understanding of the paranormal mobilized here, is situated between postcolonial hybridity and decolonial nationalism, it is actually incommensurate with my reading of Arimah. First, Cooper's interpretative gesture mobilizes colonialism and elides transatlantic slavery as the *primal scene* of Africa. This historical truncation serves to elide the continuities that precipitated the transition from slavery to colonialism. Second, Copper's insistence on the term *magical realism* acts as an imposition on these texts. While Copper goes to great lengths to historize and theorize her use of the term, magical realism cannot shake its supplement. It acts as an epistemological othering that locates these texts simultaneously within the world of the superstitious and the magical as well as Copper's "third space." Third, the paranormal that I mobilize here is less invested in the possibilities of a third space, and more interested in how these parallel and ancillary modes of reading necessitate an interrogation of the conceptual and interpretive frames that cohere literature by African and African-descended writers. In this way I also diverge from Garuba's understanding of magical realism as a subcategory of animist realism, which is itself a category of animist materialism.[55]

One way the paranormal troubles Cooper's reading of West African fiction within the framework of magical realism is that it calls for a rethinking of the bifurcation between science and technology, on the one hand, and animism and magic, on the other. Here we might ask: In what ways does bifurcating science fiction from magical realism or from animism emphasize the distinction that what Euro-American writers do is science fiction, and what non-Euro-American writers create is magical or animist? What would it mean to read Arimah's narratives as science fiction, animist, *and* magical? One way forward is to attend to the critique of science, technology, and innovation (STI) as mimicking global structures of power that elide Africa's role in these. Mavhunga argues that the history and structure of global power means that the definition of STI consists of concepts that have been inseparable from the colonial project.[56] The definition and methodologies that make up STI limit its scope to places beyond the African continent. Mavhunga contends that "Africa must be willing to chart a different STI and development trajectory and devise its own measurement, rather than slavishly following the Oslo or Frascati manuals, which Latin American countries have left behind in favor of their own Bogota manual."[57] This new instantiation of STI must also permit a recalibration of the segregation of "magical realism" from the categories of science fiction, for instance. With regard to Mavhunga, we might ask, How is the persisting framing of Africa (ns) as a consumer of Western technology and innovation disrupted by the narrative spaces such as those created by Arimah? And how do we reconcile Arimah's entwinement of the formation of worlds that are simultaneously magical, mythical, scientific, and speculative?

Arimah's story "Who Will Greet You at Home," for instance, entwines scientific invention and reproduction with mythmaking and magic, even as it describes the social pressure to reproduce that Nigerian woman encounter.[58] In this story the main character, Ogechi, lives in a predominantly female world where women reproduce asexually by creating their children out of materials available to them. This form of reproduction, depicted through Ogechi, an assistant at a hair salon, foregrounds class and access to material resources as the determinant of the material and character of one's child. The story critiques how human sexual reproduction is often the sole burden of women. Sexual reproduction in humans requires fertilization of an egg by a sperm, a gestation period of about nine months, and a further period of care for the child, which often falls disproportionately on women. In the story, it is the women who must create their children. And women like Ogechi, working-class women with limited access to certain materials, must fashion a child out of the resources readily available to them. The various materials from which Ogechi and the other women in the story create their children (yarn, raffia, porcelain, paper, etc.) become symbolic of the children's characters and mannerisms once they become animated. For instance, when Ogechi takes a child made from cotton tufts to her mother, she is rebuked and told, "This thing will grow fat and useless," and later, when she takes a child made of wrapping paper, her mother "plunged it into the mop bucket until it softened and fell apart."[59] Similarly, when Ogechi meets a woman with a porcelain baby in a "frilly white dress and frilly socks and soft-soled shoes," she avers, "Only a very wealthy and lucky woman would be able to keep such a delicate thing unbroken for the full year it would take before the child became flesh."[60] The materials from which children are fashioned signal their class and privilege, as well as the characteristics they are likely to be imbued with. The relationship between material and character constitutes a continuum in this world where the parent's past and present literally form the child's future.

The various materials from which children are fashioned also gesture toward Indigenous skills and innovations. While on the bus, Ogechi encounters two basket weavers who have woven their children out of raffia: "One had plain raffia streaked with blues and greens, while the other's baby was entirely red, and every passenger admired them. They would grow up to be tough and bright and skilled."[61] Raffia, a plant native to sub-Saharan Africa, is widely used around the world to make rope, baskets, placemats, hats, shoes, and textiles. Raffia contains resin, which makes it more pliable than straw. While raffia has been used by Indigenous people across Africa to make baskets, mats, and other household products, in "Who Will Greet You at Home" that innovation and skill is extended to the making of children. The training required to be an expert basket weaver forms part of the innovation that is often unrecognized because of how language as an imperial imposition continues, as Mavhunga argues, to frame our understanding of what constitutes innovation. The translation of the weavers' skills to the creation of a child, though brief, exemplifies what Geri Augusto describes as a "recombination or cumulative synthesis" where existing processes and technologies "recombine" in innovative ways.[62] The innovations and transformations through which artisans and people across the African continent and the diaspora address their particular needs and aspirations should be folded into the discourse of science and technology. What I am getting at here is that by reading "Who Will Greet You at Home" through the valence offered by African science and technology, for instance, the obvious innovations and technologies that these women employ to fashion their children become part of the interpretive framework. However, if we stay solely within the generic framing of magical realism, the designation "magical" reduces these skills and innovation to something strange and unknown that can only be interpreted as such. It is, rather, in exceeding the magical, stretching it toward something like the paranormal, that the parallels between technique and technological innovation can be rendered visible.

An example of this paranormal excess is Ogechi's determination to reproduce only if the child would be a fitting substitute for the parts of herself that will be excised by raising a child.[63] This framing of excision rather than supplement intervenes in the popular discourse of reproduction as adding something to one's life. While this determination leads to Ogechi's estrangement from her mother and an exploitative relationship with her boss, it frames reproduction away from the discourse of duty and expectation, toward one of exchange. What Ogechi ostensibly undertakes is a renegotiation of the normative or the assumptive logic for reproduction. For Ogechi, this negotiation hinges on the formation of a child with the requisite material that will result in a delicate and "perfect" child worthy of her sacrifices. Ogechi herself was born to a poor mother who fashioned her out of twigs and mud and wrapped her tightly in leaves. Thus Ogechi's repeated rejection of her mother's suggestion to form her child using the same materials implies that Ogechi finds in her current condition a correlation between being formed from mud, twigs, and leaves and being a poor apprentice who must sell her joy and empathy to survive. Thus the materials she chooses, though capable of weaving a child, are impermanent, fragile, and, interestingly, likely to be imported from elsewhere in the world.

For instance, Ogechi makes a child out of yarn that "lasted a good month, emitting dry, cotton-soft gurgles and pooping little balls of lint, before Ogechi snagged its thigh on a nail and it unraveled as she continued to walk." Faced with the destruction of another child before they reach the gestational period of a year, Ogechi reasons that a mother who takes "danfo to work if she had money, walked if she didn't, and lived in an apartment that amounted to a room she could clear in three large steps" should have known better than to use yarn to fashion a child.[64] Ultimately Ogechi, in her desperation for a child, weaves one out of hair. When this child develops a taste for human blood, Ogechi saves herself from the child by burning it, then forms a new child from the ashes. That Ogechi's attempts to renegotiate with the normative structures fail is inevitable, yet she does fashion a child from materials (hair and shampoo) that are beyond her means. Instead of resisting or opposing the normative structures, Ogechi fashions a paranormal space within which she can re-create the blood-hungry child into one refashioned from the ashes of the old. That the baby made from hair is burned and a new one is formed from its ashes suggests not a repurposing of the old but an actual (scientifically defined) transformation. Within this paranormal space, Ogechi's new child bears "her mother's face," and its joy is its only currency. Ogechi chants as she molds her new child, "*Let this child be born in sorrow. . . . Let this child live in sorrow. Let this child not grow into a foolish, hopeful girl with joy to barter.*"[65] Realizing that her child cannot have a life so radically distinct from hers, because the world she inhabits has not fundamentally changed, Ogechi creates a child who will not trade her joy as currency with which to mobilize her own desires, aspirations, and failures.

The things that Ogechi gives up (or rather the things that are taken from her), in her quest to have the perfect child, connect "Who Will Greet You at Home" to the eponymous story of the collection, "What It Means." Mama, the owner of the emporium where Ogechi works as an assistant hairdresser, siphons Ogechi's joy and empathy as payment for blessing her child and as rent for Ogechi's apartment. As Ogechi states: "The woman had already taken most of her empathy, so that she found herself spitting in the palms of beggars. She'd started on joy the last time, agreeing to bless the yarn baby. All that empathy and joy and who knows what else Mama took from her and the other desperate girls who visited her back room kept her blessing active long past when it should have faded."[66] The means of exploitation, as Ogechi describes, exceeds the material and structural dispossessions that keep the poor perpetually indebted, by transgressing into a metaphysical where one utilizes one's emotions as currency. Tyrone Palmer's critique of Black affect as "*unthinkable*, falling within the epistemological closure of Man's episteme; buried beneath an overdetermined discourse that reads the expression and performance of Black affect as always already excessive, inadequate, or both" is thus particularly poignant.[67] Palmer explicates Sylvia Wynter's framing of the "extreme epistemological and metaphysical violence" that is Western modernity and its instantiation of humanity by which "the Black is positioned as the constitutive outside of the Human."[68] Though Palmer centers his theorization of the "unthinkability of Black affect" on Claudia

Rankine's *Citizen*, there exist significant parallels between his observation that Black affect always already embodies a disfiguring of the reach and scope of affect, on the one hand, and the ways the siphoning of Ogechi's joy and empathy manifests itself, on the other. Mama's siphoning of Ogechi's joy and empathy catalyzes certain reactions in her (such as spitting in the palms of beggars) that exemplify Ogechi's unimaginable suffering, which is unrecognizable in her actions. Ogechi's suffering is coded in the very fabric of Black being, and although this suffering is in the fabric of the world, it becomes material enough to be mobilized only when it is filtered through economic exchange. The paranormal, here, erects a barrier that, while allowing us to see the immaterial dispossession that is the condition of Ogechi's life, negates any interpretation of her affect as a visible signifier of her interiority. The evidence of Ogechi's suffering exists beyond her affective response; indeed, it is unthinkable and unrecognizable.

Conclusion

> By way of contrast, the Frantz Fanon of *Black Skin, White Masks* hits upon (but is never quite comfortable with) the idea that the violence Black people face is a violence of a parallel universe. In short, Black people and non-Black people do not exist in the same universe or paradigm of violence, any more than fish and birds exist in the same region of the world.
> —Frank Wilderson III, *Afropessimism*

In a *New York Times* article titled "A Warning That Africa's Last Glaciers Will Soon Vanish," Marc Santora reports that even though Africa contributes less than 4 percent to the global greenhouse gas emission, the continent will suffer an "outsized impact" if the current rate of climate warming continues. Drawing on the example of Mount Kenya, the article states, "The glacier of Mount Kenya . . . is expected to be gone a decade sooner."[69] Though the article is informative, it repeats with precision the sort of reporting about Africa that provides information about the entire continent without speaking to or getting a response from anyone from Africa. The creation and invention of knowledge about Africa is nothing new, and what Santora's article and countless others do is echo the assumption that Africans have nothing to contribute to the conversation on climate change and no coherent response to it that warrants inclusion in the pages of the *New York Times*.[70] Indeed, in the aftermath of the recently concluded 2021 United Nations Climate Change Conference in Glasgow, the Kenyan environment minister, Keriako Tobiko, pointed out that capping global climate heating at 1.5 degrees Celsius does not consider the uneven and unequal heating across the globe. According to Tobiko, a 1.5 degree increase in global climate temperature is equivalent to more than 3.0 degrees across the African continent.[71] The assumed equivalence of global climate continues to the environmental transformation that a heating climate engenders across the African continent. This is perhaps only one example of the different paradigms that structure the lives of Black people in Africa and in the world, what Frank Wilderson III asserts as the "parallel universe" in which Black people live.[72] That these universes and worlds are paranormal is what I have tried to suggest through the work of Arimah. These paranormal structures, whether framed within the continuum of violence or within the technological innovations that are excised from the domain of science and technology and fixed in magical realism, exist to reveal the cracks in the world and its unease with Blackness.

What is further unraveled in Arimah's short stories are these violent ties that bind ever tightly the political, economic, and social structures of the postcolony, for instance, to the ever-present possibility of return to the colonial framework. This essay positions the endurance of the regimes of colonial structures and epistemologies as the foundation of the normative, and the moments of seeming transformation, such as independence, as the paranormal—as the distortion of the system that can be seen yet cannot be made real.[73] The core concerns of this essay are the interplay between space and time, between a persistent structure that innovates and conceals its workings, and an imagined future that predicts its instantiation at the expense of those caught within its matrix. These continuums cannot be examined within the progressivist temporality of modernity, but their futural instantiation in Arimah's para-worlds permits their closer interrogation.

....

DELALI KUMAVIE is assistant professor in the Department of English at Syracuse University. Her current research project examines the intersection of Blackness, aviation, and literature. She has published or has pieces forthcoming in *Feminist Africa*, *Substance*, *Propter Nos*, *Postcolonial Text*, and *English Language Notes*.

Acknowledgments

I am grateful to Ethan Madarieta, Carol Fadda, and the editorial board of *Qui Parle* for their thoughtful insights and comments on earlier versions of this essay.

Notes

1. In using *common sense*, I am following Saidiya V. Hartman's use of the term in *Scenes of Subjection*, where Hartman distills from Gramsci's term a challenge to the normative accounts of slavery and freedom. Hartman writes about Gramsci's concept of common sense as "a conception of world and life 'implicit to a large extent in determinate strata of society' and 'in opposition to "official" conceptions of the world.'" In Hartman's use of the term, common sense "challenges the official accounts of freedom and stresses the similarities and correspondences of slavery and freedom. At a minimum, these observations disclose the disavowed transactions between slavery and freedom as modes of production and subjection." See Hartman, *Scenes of Subjection*, 13.
2. Seaman, "What It Means," 21.
3. McCain, "Postcolonial Mythologies," 7.
4. Treisman, "Lesley Nneka Arimah."
5. Treisman, "Lesley Nneka Arimah."
6. McCain, "Postcolonial Mythologies," 7.
7. McCain, "Postcolonial Mythologies," 7.
8. Garuba, "On Animism," 8.
9. Mavhunga, "Introduction," 1.
10. Garuba, "Explorations in Animist Materialism," 267.
11. Garuba, "Explorations in Animist Materialism," 273–74.
12. Garuba, "Explorations in Animist Materialism," 274.
13. Fanon, *Black Skin, White Masks*, 21.

14. According to Roland Barthes, myth is a peculiar system because it is constructed from a semiological chain that existed before it: it is a second-order semiological system. What is a sign in the first system becomes a mere signifier in the second. We must here recall that the materials of mythical speech (the language itself, photography, painting, posters, rituals, objects, etc.), however different at the start, are reduced to a pure signifying function as soon as they are caught by myth. Myth sees in them only the same raw material; their unity is that they all come down to the status of a mere language. Whether it deals with alphabetical or pictorial writing, myth wants to see in them only a sum of signs, a global sign, and the final term of a first semiological chain. Barthes's myth constitutes a second-tier signifier by which new, culturally specific meanings and/or narratives become intwined with the sign, such as race becoming attached to skin color or what Fanon calls the "epidermal racial schema." See Barthes, *Mythologies*; and Fanon, *Black Skin, White Masks*.

15. Marriott, *Whither Fanon?*, 89–90.

16. Marriott, *Whither Fanon?*, 90.

17. Marriott, *Whither Fanon?*, 91.

18. African literary scholars such as Ato Quayson have long argued that interpretation of African literature focused either on its unique aesthetics or on the documentary evidence it provided ("Incessant Particularities," 123–24).

19. Garuba, "Explorations in Animist Materialism," 274–75.

20. Mavhunga, "Introduction," 7.

21. Sexton, "Afro-Pessimism."

22. *Oxford English Dictionary*, www.oed.com, s.v. "para-," def. 1.

23. It is in this sense that we get words like *paraphysical*, "not part of the physical world as it is currently understood; of, relating to, or designating physical phenomena for which no adequate scientific explanation exists." *Para* functions similarly in words like *parapolitical*, "existing parallel to, or outside, the sphere of mainstream (esp. national) politics" (*Oxford English Dictionary*, s.vv. "paraphysical," "parapolitical").

24. Using Hortense Spillers's concept of vestibularity, which appropriates an architectural term that denotes a passageway or a threshold on which to position the Black female body as the entryway into the violence endemic to Blackness in the world.

25. *Oxford English Dictionary*, s.vv. "parasol," "paravent," "parapet."

26. *Oxford English Dictionary*, s.v. "paranormal."
27. Wiegman and Wilson, "Introduction," 5.
28. Wiegman and Wilson, "Introduction," 6–7.
29. Wiegman and Wilson, "Introduction," 17.
30. Wiegman and Wilson, "Introduction," 17–18.
31. Hartman, *Scenes of Subjection*, 34.
32. Hartman, *Scenes of Subjection*, 34–35.
33. Getachew, *Worldmaking after Empire*, 3.
34. Jackson, *Becoming Human*, 45.
35. These are mere examples of a vast array of literary texts that and writers who can be included in this category. See Aidoo, *Our Sister Killjoy*; Achebe, *A Man of the People*; and Ngugi, *A Grain of Wheat*.
36. Borzutzky, "talk to me about translation," 22.
37. Karera, "Blackness and the Pitfalls of Anthropocene Ethics," 34.
38. Karera, "Blackness and the Pitfalls of Anthropocene Ethics," 51.
39. Fanon, *Black Skin, White Masks*, 92.
40. Arimah, "What It Means," 166.
41. Arimah, "What It Means," 156.
42. Arimah, "What It Means," 159.
43. Wilderson, *Red, White, and Black*, 18.
44. Arimah, "What It Means," 160.
45. Arimah, "What It Means," 161.
46. Warren, "Catastrophe," 354.
47. Warren, "Catastrophe," 358.
48. Arimah, "What It Means," 173–74.
49. Arimah, "What It Means," 174.
50. Cooper, *Magical Realism in West African Fiction*, 17.
51. Cooper, *Magical Realism in West African Fiction*, 1.
52. Cooper, *Magical Realism in West African Fiction*, 36.
53. Cooper, *Magical Realism in West African Fiction*, 36.
54. Cooper, *Magical Realism in West African Fiction*, 216. Olatubosun Ogunsanwo, in his review of Cooper's book, asks if the term *magical realism* is a "serious misnomer" for the book's analysis of syncreticity ("Magical Realism in West African Fiction").
55. Garuba, "Explorations in Animist Materialism," 275.
56. Mavhunga, "Introduction," 5.
57. Mavhunga, "Introduction," 27.
58. Treisman, "Lesley Nneka Arimah."
59. Arimah, "Who Will Greet You at Home," 96.
60. Arimah, "Who Will Greet You at Home," 99.
61. Arimah, "Who Will Greet You at Home," 95.

62. Augusto, "Plants of Bondage," 82. D. A. Masolo also proposes that we consider the transformation of the mobile phone across Africa through telephone or mobile banking applications, long before it became a feature of mobile phones in the United States, as an "African technological tool." Masolo explains that "ingenuity includes intellectual perceptivity that allows one to see possible adaptations to a tool already in existence" ("The Place of Science and Technology in Our Lives," 36).

63. Arimah, "Who Will Greet You at Home," 95.

64. Arimah, "Who Will Greet You at Home," 93, 94.

65. Arimah, "Who Will Greet You at Home," 121.

66. Arimah, "Who Will Greet You at Home," 98–99.

67. Palmer, "'What Feels More Than Feeling?,'" 33.

68. Palmer, "'What Feels More Than Feeling?,'" 32. See also Wynter, "1492."

69. Santora, "A Warning That Africa's Last Glacier Will Soon Vanish."

70. See Mudimbe, *Invention of Africa*, for an expansive analysis of Africa in relation to discursive and epistemological formations.

71. Tobiko, "COP26 Ministerial Dialogue on Adaptation Action," 26:13.

72. Wilderson, *Afropessimism*, 240.

73. For further examination of the persistent remains of colonial epistemologies, see Coly, *Postcolonial Hauntologies*.

References

Achebe, Chinua. *A Man of the People*. Harlow: Heinemann, 1966.

Aidoo, Ama Ata. *Our Sister Killjoy*. Harlow: Pearson Education, 1977.

Arimah, Lesley Nneka. "What It Means When a Man Falls from the Sky." In Arimah, *What It Means When a Man Falls from the Sky*, 151–74.

Arimah, Lesley Nneka. *What It Means When a Man Falls from the Sky*. New York: Riverhead, 2017.

Augusto, Geri. "Plants of Bondage, Limbo Plants, and Liberation Flora: Diasporic Reflections for STS in Africa and Africa in STS." In *What Do Science, Technology, and Innovation Mean from Africa?*, edited by Clapperton Chakanetsa Mavhunga, 79–95. Cambridge, MA: MIT Press, 2017.

Barthes, Roland. *Mythologies*, translated by Annette Lavers. New York: Hill and Wang, 1972.

Borzutzky, Daniel. "talk to me about translation: a broken introduction." In *Memories of My Overdevelopment*, 19–24. Chicago: Kenning, 2015.

Coly, Ayo A. *Postcolonial Hauntologies: African Women's Discourses of the Female Body*. Lincoln: University of Nebraska Press, 2019.

Cooper, Brenda. *Magical Realism in West African Fiction: Seeing with a Third Eye*. London: Routledge, 1998.

Fanon, Frantz. *Black Skin, White Masks*, translated by Richard Philcox. New York: Grove, 1991.

Garuba, Harry. "Explorations in Animist Materialism: Notes on Reading/Writing African Literature, Culture, and Society." *Public Culture* 15, no. 2 (2003): 261–86.

Garuba, Harry. "On Animism, Modernity/Colonialism, and the African Order of Knowledge: Provisional Reflections." *e-flux Journal*, no. 36 (2012). www.e-flux.com/journal/36/61249/on-animism-modernity-colonialism-and-the-african-order-of-knowledge-provisional-reflections.

Getachew, Adom. *Worldmaking after Empire: The Rise and Fall of Self-Determination*. Princeton, NJ: Princeton University Press, 2019.

Hartman, Saidiya V. *Scenes of Subjection: Terror, Slavery, and Self-Making in Nineteenth-Century America*. New York: Oxford University Press, 1997.

Jackson, Zakiyyah Iman. *Becoming Human: Matter and Meaning in an Antiblack World*. New York: New York University Press, 2020.

Karera, Axelle. "Blackness and the Pitfalls of Anthropocene Ethics." *Critical Philosophy of Race* 7, no. 1 (2019): 32–56.

Marriott, David. *Whither Fanon? Studies in the Blackness of Being*. Stanford, CA: Stanford University Press, 2018.

Masolo, D. A. "The Place of Science and Technology in Our Lives: Making Sense of Possibilities." In *What Do Science, Technology, and Innovation Mean from Africa?*, edited by Clapperton Chakanetsa Mavhunga, 29–44. Cambridge, MA: MIT Press, 2017.

Mavhunga, Clapperton Chakanetsa. "Introduction: What Do Science, Technology, and Innovation Mean from Africa?" In *What Do Science, Technology, and Innovation Mean from Africa?*, edited by Clapperton Chakanetsa Mavhunga, 1–27. Cambridge, MA: MIT Press, 2017.

McCain, Carmen. "Postcolonial Mythologies." *American Book Review* 39, no. 4 (2018): 7–8.

Mudimbe, V. Y. *The Invention of Africa: Gnosis, Philosophy, and the Order of Knowledge*. Bloomington: Indiana University Press, 1988.

Ngũgĩ wa Thiong'o. *A Grain of Wheat*. London: Heinemann, 1967.

Ogunsanwo, Olatubosun. "Magical Realism in West African Fiction: Seeing with a Third Eye." Review of *Magical Realism in West African Fiction: Seeing with a Third Eye*, by Brenda Cooper. *Research in African Literature* 31, no. 2 (2000): 226–28.

Palmer, Tyrone S. "'What Feels More Than Feeling?': Theorizing the Unthinkability of Black Affect." *Critical Ethnic Studies* 3, no. 2 (2017): 31–56.

Quayson, Ato. "Incessant Particularities: 'Calibrations' as Close Reading." *Research in African Literature* 36, no. 2 (2005): 122–31.

Santora, Marc. "A Warning That Africa's Last Glacier Will Soon Vanish." *New York Times*, October 19, 2021. www.nytimes.com/2021/10/19 /world/africa/mountain-glaciers-disappear.html.

Seaman, Donna. "What It Means When a Man Falls from the Sky." Review of *What It Means When a Man Falls from the Sky*, by Lesley Nneka Arimah. *American Library Association*, March 15, 2017.

Sexton, Jared. "Afro-Pessimism: The Unclear Word." *Rhizomes*, no. 29 (2016). www.rhizomes.net/issue29/sexton.html.

Spillers, Hortense. "Mama's Baby, Papa's Maybe: An American Grammar Book." In *Black, White, and in Color: Essays on American literature and Culture*, 203–29. Chicago: University of Chicago Press, 2003.

Tobiko, Keriako. "COP26 Ministerial Dialogue on Adaptation Action." United Nations Climate Change Conference, Glasgow. Posted November 9, 2021. www.youtube.com/watch?v=7QVS7BB44vI.

Treisman, Deborah. "Lesley Nneka Arimah: On Imagining a Universe of Handcrafted Babies." *New Yorker*, October 19, 2015. www.newyorker .com/books/page-turner/fiction-this-week-lesley-nneka-arimah-2015 -10-26.

Warren, Calvin. "The Catastrophe: Black Feminist Poethics, (Anti)form, and Mathematical Nihilism." *Qui Parle* 28, no. 2 (2019): 353–72.

Wiegman, Robyn, and Elizabeth A. Wilson. "Introduction: Antinormativity's Queer Conventions." *differences* 26, no. 1 (2015): 1–25.

Wilderson, Frank B., III. *Red, White, and Black: Cinema and the Structure of U.S. Antagonisms*. Durham, NC: Duke University Press, 2010.

Wilderson, Frank B., III. *Afropessimism*. New York: Liveright, 2018.

Wynter, Sylvia. "1492: A New World View." In *Race, Discourse, and the Origin of the Americas: A New World View*, edited by Vera Lawrence Hyatt and Rex M. Nettleford, 5–57. Washington, DC: Smithsonian Institution Press, 1995.

The Devil Finds Use

Black Queers Do The Exorcist

BRANDON S. CALLENDER

Much of black horror studies today is premised on the assumption that true horror, for the black audience, is found not in the paranormal but in the normal and the systemic.[1] It is now conventional, for instance, for scholars to preface their research with a personal anecdote that swaps out a supernatural on-screen threat for a more pressing—and more horrifying—social one. Certain objects of study readily accommodate these claims, like Toni Morrison's *Beloved* or the films of Jordan Peele, while others do so only coincidentally, like *Night of the Living Dead*. Such anecdotes have helped produce a seeming consensus about where the greater horror lies for black artists and audiences. Though no black horror studies scholar cites him, the claim that the horrors of real life exceed those of the horror film actually originates in James Baldwin's searing critique of *The Exorcist* (1973) in his long essay on Hollywood cinema, *The Devil Finds Work* (1976). In the first half of this essay, I summarize the black-life-as-horror thesis to trace its lineage back to Baldwin. In the second half I depart from this thesis to offer a more capacious account of black horror spectatorship that need not maintain a traumatized

QUI PARLE   Vol. 31, No. 1, June 2022
DOI 10.1215/10418385-9669492   © 2022 Editorial Board, *Qui Parle*

fixation on a more horrifying real. Although I understand the political importance that such trauma-based claims have, the way that they naturalize black life as a collectively shared horror is too sweeping. As Kinitra D. Brooks argues, "In too many instances, horror texts have been subject to the privileging of the horror of trauma above the specific genre of horror."[2] Reading only for collective traumas erases the idiosyncratic and even playful attachments that black viewers cultivate toward horror, as evidenced in the work of three contemporary black gay authors: Larry Duplechan, James Earl Hardy, and G. Winston James. How might these campy allusions to *The Exorcist* activate new ways of seeing the film and new ways of articulating the many affective and political uses that horror has for black artists and fans? By setting their perverse delight in *The Exorcist* against Baldwin's larger rebuke of the film, I model an alternative investment black fans can have in the horror genre that does not prioritize the traumatic real.

What's Horrifying in Black Studies

For Linda Williams, the horror genre is taken to be a "low genre" because it is a "body genre," provoking bodily responses over thought. As scholars have noted, horror relies on our ability to be shocked or grossed out in ways that mimic character responses on-screen: when they scream, we scream.[3] This universal account of horror reception does less to explain the more particular ways that black subjects narrate their own visceral and psychological responses to the genre. For the leading voices of black horror today—including fiction writers such as Tananarive Due, Walidah Imarisha, and Victor LaValle and scholars such as Robin R. Coleman, Maisha L. Wester, and Leila Taylor—the visceral feeling of horror depends more on racial triggers than on the otherworldly frights. For instance, in a foundational work of black horror studies, *Horror Noire* (2011), Coleman recalls how the zombies from *Night of the Living Dead* were far less frightening than the trigger-happy white mob who arrive at the film's conclusion and fatally mistake the black lead for a zombie. While the director never intended for race to be meaningful, its impact on black audience members was enough to usurp the film's intended horror.

Coleman's takeaway—"In the real world of Black men White mobs are far more deadly"—has helped establish a narrative about how black fans really regard such otherworldly horrors: as far less terrifying than their everyday lives.[4] Her account neatly exemplifies the powerfully disjunctive way that black subjects enter into the horror genre by disidentifying with horror itself. As José Esteban Muñoz theorizes, "To disidentify is to read oneself and one's own life narrative in a moment, object, or subject that is not culturally coded to 'connect' with the disidentifying subject."[5] These reading strategies ensure that black subjects can experience racially affirming connections both with and within the horror genre even when they are least intended to do so. Moreover, disidentification disrupts how horror both markets and identifies itself. The horror genre may be named after the very emotion that it hopes to provoke in its audience, but the leading voices of black horror today never rightly experience those horrors most intended by the genre.[6]

By swapping out superficial horrors for social ones, black subjects today enter into the horror genre as its rivals, if not its foils. Instead of reeling from horror's intended "dreadful pleasures," they experience a horror that arises more traumatically, more personally, and more incidentally as a result of their racial consciousness. Walidah Imarisha thus begins her introduction to the 2017 landmark anthology of black women's horror stories, *Sycorax's Daughters*, with the declaration that "devils and vampires are almost banal" when compared with the lived experiences of black people, especially "the ultimate horror story, slavery."[7] Taylor similarly begins her essay collection, *Darkly* (2019), with the memory of a tour guide on a haunted plantation who astutely replaced all the usual ghost yarns with quotidian histories of black suffering: "But as the tour guide understood, America's haunted history is Black history."[8] In such cases, black subjects can establish a strong affinity with the genre in ways that have little to do with its intended forms of reception.

Without delving too deeply into the black horror literary tradition, I will only note that the most acclaimed voices of literary horror today also tend to elevate the everyday horrors of black life over otherworldly ones. At the top of this list are Victor LaValle's *Ballad of Black Tom* (2016) and Matt Ruff's *Lovecraft Country* (2016), two

Lovecraftian novels that rely on the premise that normal life for a black person is far more frightening than anything Lovecraft could have dreamed up. LaValle powerfully makes this point when he has his black protagonist grudgingly state his preference for battling Lovecraftian gods over the more frightening everyday world of white supremacy: "*I'll take Cthulhu over you devils any day.*"[9]

Yet there are just as many depictions of black horror fans as recreationally turning to the genre as an empty, trigger-free pleasure. If the real world intrudes on them in any way, it is only as an obligation: a felt shame that by watching and reading horror they are shirking the responsibility to confront the reality of race. In one especially poignant example—Tananarive Due's possession thriller, *The Good House* (2003)—Due's protagonist uneasily admits to preferring supernatural thrillers to a black realist canon, epitomized by Baldwin. Confronting the horrors of black life seems more like a grudging necessity that exists totally separate from the relief that horror affords him: "With so much to learn about the real world, how could he justify wasting hours wandering through the realms of make-believe? With so many real problems, he'd never had time to care about the imaginary ones."[10] His vexed articulation of horror fandom powerfully intervenes into our fixed doxa about how black subjects experience the horror of the horror film. From this perspective, we cannot take it for granted that black horror fans are always processing and prioritizing the greater horrors of black life. Horror is instead valuable because it grants a reprieve from having to confront the weightier meaning that race assumes within the real world.

I say this to risk a simple point: the horror that black fans experience cannot always be explained by recourse to a singular collective trauma. The importance of black horror studies as a field need not come at the expense of these more recreational, more generic, more wayward pleasures. Whether experienced innately or as an external imperative, such accounts ensure that recreational terrors matter for the black viewer only insofar as they confront the collective trauma that black people face daily. I am troubled by these accounts because they occlude other forms of reception. The danger of this story—a single story—is that it tends to naturalize how black fans are expected to see themselves in horror. Moreover, it tends to naturalize black life *as horror*. It does so by erasing entirely the possibility of reprieve—and pleasure—and insisting that black audiences have no other way into the genre than through traumas that they are always said to be processing. We are left with only one imperative: black horror simply cannot—*must not*—lose its grip on its greater and more horrifying knowledge of the real. It must face in everything the devil we know—the horrors of normal life—rather than those imagined forces that we have no right to fear.

I argue not that we should let go of this approach altogether but that we might do more to conceptualize the multiple ways black fans find pleasure in horror films that have no clear relation to the story of black life as the greater horror. In a moment where the market is turning more to social horror films that explicitly tackle racism, my interest in what *The Exorcist* means to black audiences hopes to ignite a critical interest in horror films that as yet have no readily available place within black study. I look to *The Exorcist*—rather than its Blaxploitation remake, *Abby* (1975)—because it illuminates the complex identifications that black subjects continue to have with white mainstream horror films. For this same reason I do not locate the meaning that possession has within black studies through its two more likely candidates: the "voodoo" film and the vodun religion that it maligns. Instead, I look to the paranormal antics of *The Exorcist*'s possessed child, Regan, because I want to take seriously what the generic thrills of the possession film can offer black audiences beyond yet another sobering encounter with the real.

Opening Night: *The Exorcist* and Black Studies

In his foundational study *The Philosophy of Horror* (1990), Noël Carroll suggests that perhaps it is only through our willing "suspension of disbelief" that we can experience that same fear which characters on-screen feel toward otherworldly horrors.[11] Baldwin's own account of such openness problematizes this account of reception. Carroll may be terrified by otherworldly horrors like *The Exorcist*, but Baldwin suggests that black viewers cannot entertain these same generic frights as easily because they can never suspend their knowledge, and dread, of the real. Though Baldwin tries hard to play along with *The Exorcist*—"I saw the film again, alone. I tried to be absolutely open to it, suspending judgment as totally as I could"—his racial consciousness as a black subject prohibits him from doing so.[12]

Baldwin's closed response has a powerful and understudied importance within the less racially literate field of horror studies. Specifically, his inability to remain "absolutely open" to *The Exorcist* here undercuts a powerful voice in horror studies: Carol J. Clover's landmark study *Men, Women, and Chainsaws* (1992). In her chapter on the possession film, "Opening Up," Clover uses this phrase to dramatize and critique the gendered politics of the possession film. She reads into the subgenre a gendered tension between two warring epistemes: masculine reason ("white science") and feminized faith ("black magic").[13] Elevating gender-based analysis over the racial salience of her terms, Clover uses them to incisively argue that possession films dramatize the need for rigid men to "open up" to this superstition that they abject onto women. She rightly points out that *The Exorcist* is not really about the possessed child, but about her ability to win over those who were falling away from faith both in and out of the film. The film itself centers around the attempts of a single mother, Chris MacNeil, to save her violently possessed daughter, Regan, from her lewdly destructive behaviors. To do so, Chris must renounce medicine and psychology's diagnostic powers ("white science") and instead embrace the more antiquated practices of the church ("black magic"). Regan is ultimately cured when Chris gets a jaded pastor, Father Karras, to perform an exorcism that he at first doesn't believe in but that eventually strengthens his faith. Within the film, possession is a performance the devil stages to provoke a loss of faith in his audience. Outside the film, however, it is a performance staged by the film (and the novel it is based on) to do the opposite: lead the wayward back to faith. Audiences are meant, like Karras, to open up. Spectacularly, they do.

Though Clover's gender-based claims are powerful, her racially salient yet largely colorblind categories of "white science" and "black magic" do less to explain why Baldwin, as a black person, is himself kept from "opening up" to the film's message. His racial difference introduces into Clover's framework a critical disposition that she nowhere anticipates. His racial difference leaves him indifferent to the film's intended horrors. He is open neither to its message nor to what Adam Charles Hart refers to as the "sensational address" of the horror film—its ability to excite in the viewer's body those same fear responses that characters portray on-screen.[14] We can contrast Baldwin's coolness—his closedness—with the infamous hype that the film generated. As Adam Rockoff recalls, "When it was originally released in 1973 . . . many in the audience vomited. Some fainted. Others had to seek therapy or religious counsel."[15] Such hysterics bothered Baldwin. If Regan's wildly vomiting body proves that she is possessed, then those of the audience members proved that they were equally possessed by the rising power of faith. Fearing the film's hold over its audience, Baldwin pens a corrective that shifts the source of terror from the possessed child to the normative social body that fights to reclaim her. In a clever act of disidentification and displacement, he routes the language of terror from the demonic to the more insidious world of white normativity that dissembles its wickedness:

> The mindless and hysterical banality of the evil presented in *The Exorcist* is the most terrifying thing about the film. The Americans should certainly know more about evil than that; if they pretend otherwise, they are lying, and any black man, and not only blacks— many, many others, including white children—can call them on this lie; he who has been treated *as* the devil recognizes the devil when they meet. (*DFW*, 126)

Baldwin concentrates most of his ire on Chris, whose job as an actress helps channel his earlier critique of Hollywood as an enterprise that elevates white fantasies over reality. Chris exemplifies complacency not only in her wealth but also in the lines that she delivers as an actress at the start of the film. Getting into character, she mounts a podium to address campus protesters, demanding, "Order! Order! If you wanna effect any change you'll have to do it within the system!"[16] Even after she exits the set, Chris emblematizes for Baldwin "all of the really dreadful apathy of the American middle class" for remaining unable to confront "her guilt concerning . . . her essentially empty and hypocritical and totally unanchored life. . . . This uneasy, and even terrified guilt is the subtext of *The Exorcist*, which cannot, however, exorcise it since it never confronts it" (*DFW*, 123, 125). Her ideology thus becomes—like that of the film itself—the true devil of the film. Through this framing Baldwin usurps the film's titular hero—the exorcist—and himself becomes this heroic figure. Ideology critique *becomes* the new exorcism. It allows Baldwin to cast out the more terrifying normativity in a way that the film simply will not, even though, as Baldwin quickly notes, "this confrontation would have been to confront the devil" (*DFW*, 125).

Baldwin's "deliberate attempt to leave myself open" to *The Exorcist* and his inability to do so thus constitute a critique of the film that Clover cannot capture in her loaded binary of "white science" versus "black magic" (*DFW*, 125). Baldwin remains closed to the film's black magic simply because, as a black person, he cannot suspend his disbelief in the more insidious reality of racial capitalism. His reading shifts the onus from "opening up" to faith to falling away from it: falling away from our whitest faith in all institutions that perpetuate this killing banality. We are to see evil not as some otherworldly affliction but as inextricable from our encounters with and susceptibility to those normative ideologies that reinforce the oppressive world around us. "For, I have seen the devil by day and by night, and have seen him in you and in me," he writes, and proceeds to list cops, junkies, presidents, and, yes, even housewives and preachers (*DFW*, 126).

Baldwin twists the word *possession* in the same way he does *horrifying*, *dreadful*, and *exorcism*. He prefaces his turn to *The Exorcist* with a critique of how "the Western world pivots on the infantile, and, in action, criminal delusions of possession, and of property" (*DFW*, 120). His rage against the materialist will to possess belittles what, in his opinion, Chris most wants for her daughter: to "make as much money" as her (*DFW*, 124). Not once does Baldwin seem interested in Regan's paranormal afflictions; he cares less about her status as possessed than about her status as future *possessor*. How many lives must be dispossessed to continue that normal life that the MacNeils so yearn for? Baldwin hints at this concern when he recalls a remark that his friend makes on exiting the film: "So, we must be careful . . . lest we lose our faith—and become possessed." According to Baldwin, his friend "was no longer speaking of the film, nor was he speaking of the church" (*DFW*, 121). Passed between black people, the word *possessed* is here loaded with a knowledge of how often black people were possessed, as objects, on the pious road to white world-building. Baldwin is speaking of faith as a spiritual force that allows black subjects to persist against the normative world that has never dispossessed itself of the urge to possess black life as property, nor once stopped to consider how the systemic devaluation of black life still enables certain families, like the MacNeils, to own and pass down property, and to have so many institutions of "white science" rush to their aid when they are in crisis. In minimizing paranormal horror, Baldwin here echoes those points made by later black horror scholars. He seems to say, like LaValle's protagonist, I'll take Satan over you devils any day.

Baldwin's ideological critique of the film finds its contemporary stakes in how we understand its place within horror studies and the attempts of the franchise to update itself in our current Black Lives Matter moment. In the first season of the television series *The Exorcist* (2016), Regan has grown up into exactly the possessing subject that Baldwin abhors. Her family is once again afflicted when one of her own daughters is possessed. But by whose devil? For a moment it seems to be Baldwin's. The franchise and its mother are given a chance to exorcise their own racial guilt when Chris calls a town meeting to search for her possessed granddaughter. The ensuing scene at the podium reprises the aforementioned one where Chris—with cameras rolling—admonishes a group of student protesters to find order within the system. Here, however, white fantasy clashes with real-life black horrors as she finally confronts that guilty conscience which Baldwin says neither she nor the franchise was ever rightly able to exorcise. As she speaks into a now-real crowd, the gathering fills with black protesters who demand to know where justice is for their own slain loved ones. They demand to know why cops care more for Regan's child than for their own. A black protester articulates Baldwin's own indictment of the film: she rails that nobody cares about the slain "poor people of color, guess that don't rate with your department superintendent. I guess because we don't have any movie stars backing us. . . . Point your damn cameras in this direction, get your lights on these faces. We don't have any reward money, but they're people too."[17] For a moment, it is as if the searing disinterest that Baldwin claims black audiences felt toward the film can rise up, as critique, within its diegetic world. The command to "point your damn cameras" shifts the language of damnation from the paranormal to the interlocking cinematic and media apparatus that keeps black lives from mattering. To point those cameras where there is no money is to route the possession story from its more spectacular frights back to the systemic world, which is a daily horror for its most dispossessed. The show itself, however, fails to heed the black woman's plea, allowing the story line to disperse as easily as its most fickle crowd. Still, for a moment the racially unmarked audience of *The Exorcist* must see their ability to connect with the earlier paranormal terror of the MacNeils in terms of race. They are made to watch as black folks protest *The Exorcist* and call out—for just a few seconds—the greater and unfaced horrors of their lives. They call out their desire to appear within a genre whose prevailing mood has long been central to their lives.

Such convergences around *The Exorcist* constellate the different investments that scholars of critical race and gender studies have in the film and in its ability to dismantle—or perpetuate—harmful ideologies. And while I value the imperative to see black life as the greater horror, I have one reservation. I fear that this will become the only claim that black studies can offer to horror studies: to make black folks into its more traumatized foils; to set the encounter with the insidiously normal over that of the paranormal. Contra Baldwin, who masterfully closes down the black audience to the generic thrills of *The Exorcist*, I turn now to more playful and diffuse ways that black audiences find themselves open to it. To do so, we need not scrap Baldwin. We need only set aside Baldwin's status as the coolly detached and demystifying spectator of black realism in favor of his less-mentioned status as a perverse reader of black reality.

However conclusive Baldwin's indictment of the film may now feel, he actually regards his audience's responses with curiosity and openness, not condemnation. "When I saw the film again, I was most concerned with the audience. I wondered what they were seeing, and what it meant to them" (*DFW*, 121–22). His curiosity creates a moment of potentiality in which he suspends his initial judgment to consider instead what other ways of seeing and feeling existed at the time. To sample these other perspectives, we need only set Baldwin's

1976 essay alongside another from that year, "Return of the Repressed," by horror's most canonical critic, Robin Wood. Like Baldwin, Wood sees the devil as but a manifestation of repressed urges that we displace onto others. Unlike Baldwin, however, he seems open to the film's norm-toppling play at possession. For Wood, Regan's "violently assertive sexuality" shatteringly unleashes everything that is repressed in "this ostensibly happy, somewhat complacent surface" of the home.[18] He may not be as racially astute as Baldwin, but he takes normativity to be just as stifling. "The implication of these films," he writes, "is that the norms by which we have lived must be destroyed and a radically new form of organization (political, social, ideological, sexual) be constructed."[19] His enthusiastic openness to regarding "the devil as hero" mirrors Andrew Scahill's own queer delight in possessed children.[20] Scahill sees *The Exorcist* as able to excite "contradictory pleasures" that "allow for the expression of repressed desires that are not sanctioned in society."[21] Would knowing of this far more unruly audience for the film have changed Baldwin's perspective? As Adam Rockoff notes, audiences today may watch the film with a kind of campy irreverence. Rockoff is shocked to see how a predominantly "Hispanic" audience now "laughed when Regan's head spun around 360 degrees. They howled with glee when she projectile-vomited pea soup. . . . Watching a preteen jab a crucifix into her vagina . . . didn't seem to faze them in the least."[22] Such creatively campy and disidentifying audiences existed both then and now, and though Baldwin's starkly realist viewing practices seem to disqualify him from these looking practices, I would suggest that he is an equally perverse reader of black reality.

Smuggling Baldwin into *The Exorcist*

In *Film Blackness* Michael Boyce Gillespie challenges the idea that black film must authentically represent the realities of black viewers. Though stunningly precise, his polemic—"If we must *see* ourselves, then let it be in mirrors and not on screens"—little prepares me for Baldwin's own queer attempts to see his own self up there on the screen.[23] For all his talk of black folk's reality, Baldwin's attempts to find traces of it in films are oddly unreal. Often he finds it by look-ing at white women. Though Baldwin initially makes it seem that "no one from the world I knew had yet made an appearance on the American Screen," that world nonetheless appears everywhere due to his strange way of looking (*DFW*, 20). After summarizing white films, he often deploys his most elastic phrase—"I knew some-thing of that"—to demonstrate his ability to relate to the experience that it captures (*DFW*, 13, 14, 18, 26). This is not because there is something universal about these films but because they seem better suited to address uniquely black realities that Hollywood still cannot bear to represent. His most dramatic claims therefore do not simply identify with white films; rather, they evacuate them of their positiv-ist content altogether to insist that such all-white films are best read as black films. In this way, a film containing only white people, "for me, had not been about white people" (*DFW*, 22–23). Baldwin's ability to see himself—as a black person—in unlikely white forms is best exemplified in one especially convoluted moment that becomes the basis for queer of color critique: the moment when Baldwin latches on to Bette Davis, insisting that "she moved just like a nigger" (*DFW*, 7). I will spend some time with this moment because it allows me to model—by rereading Baldwin—exactly the kinds of idiosyncratic identifications that Baldwin otherwise loses for me when he remains closed to *The Exorcist*.

As queer film scholars have argued in work on identification, the audience is open to seeing themselves in films in more ways than any director ever intends. The scarcity of black representation equals not the impossibility of identification but its creative overflow into un-likely bodies. This openness to connection with mainstream texts is precisely why Muñoz begins his theory of disidentification with Baldwin's attachments to Davis. *Disidentifications* champions pre-cisely such "crisscrossed" ways that marginalized subjects draw ful-fillment from dominant texts that aren't coded to represent them.[24] In the following, Baldwin identifies with Davis not only because of her black movements but because her large eyes allow him to rework the shameful things his stepfather says about his own eyes to insult his mother's: "Because I sensed something menacing and unhealthy (for me, certainly) in the face on the screen, I gave Davis's skin the dead-white greenish cast of something crawling from under a rock, but I was held, just the same, by the tense intelligence of the forehead, the disaster of the lips: and when she moved, she moved just like a nigger" (*DFW*, 7). Baldwin's identification smacks of ambivalence. As Muñoz notes, this "vexed identification with Davis" offers "something both liberatory and horrible": "A black and queer belle-lettres queen such as Baldwin finds something useful in the image; a certain survival strategy is made possible via this visual disidentifcation with Bette Davis and her freakish beauty."[25] Seeing Davis on-screen triggers Baldwin's own queer inkling that "perhaps I could find a way to use my strangeness," a strangeness that has been hatefully marked, by the patriarch, as a reviled sign of his mother (*DFW*, 8). Baldwin experiences a highly personal form of significance (in her eyes) that helps activate that racially shared knowledge that he subsequently reads into her movements. He makes a similar move later when he elevates a minstrel image of a black man rolling his eyes before the police into a far more serious encounter with black life as horror: "It is also possible that their comic, bug-eyed terror contained the truth concerning a terror by which I hoped never to be engulfed" (*DFW*, 20). In such moments Baldwin can disidentify with mainstream representations to perceive starkly realistic images of black life in unlikely forms.

In looking askew at these subjects, Baldwin steals affirmation not only for himself but also for the black audiences who wish to see their own shared reality up there on the screen. Taking back this black reality from Hollywood is strange, though, because it requires us to look for its traces in the bodies of white women. Note this conflation when Baldwin looks at yet another white actress—Sylvia Sidney—who "reminded me of a colored girl, or woman—which is to say that she was the only American film actress who reminded me of reality" (*DFW*, 21). To look for black representation in this way is to let go of the notion that representation matters only in its positivist sense. It is to embrace how blackness still matters for Baldwin even when no black bodies are present on-screen. In the absence of those actual black bodies, black reality persists in his viewings as a gesture, a feeling, or a punctum that resonates with his own memories of black life. This allows him to build and affirm a sense of black reality while using idiosyncratic memories that may in fact have nothing to do with black people.

This attempt to steal such an unlikely kind of affirmation from dominant texts comes together for Baldwin in the term *smuggling*. It is the job of the black actor and audience to smuggle into Hollywood as many bits of reality as might represent and affirm black people. "Black spectators supply the sub-text—the unspoken—out of their own lives," he writes, just as actors go against "the confines of the script" to bring "hints of reality, smuggled like contraband into a maudlin tale" (*DFW*, 104–5). Actor and audience work together as fugitives to smuggle black experiences into scripts that don't represent them. They smuggle in the conditions that allow black folks to see themselves realistically up there on the screen before those conditions even exist. This is exactly what Baldwin does with Davis: he smuggles a black queer boy into a straight white woman. Though nobody has yet made the connection, this is exactly what Eve Sedgwick does with the queer reader in one section from *Tendencies* (1993) titled "Promising, Smuggling, Reading, Overreading." Sedgwick also sees straight texts as withholding an affirmation that queer children require. To get at them, she becomes the "perverse reader" who can "wrest from them sustaining news of the world, ideas, myself, and (in various senses) my kind."[26] Like Baldwin's own relationship to black reality, Sedgwick's desire to see queer realities leads her "to smuggle queer representation in where it must be smuggled."[27] With these two accounts of smuggling, I am readying myself to finally become the kind of smuggler that Baldwin both does and doesn't intend for black audiences. Paradoxically, to steal such looks as Baldwin does is in the end to steal away from him—or rather, to steal away from him the possibility of closing down black identification with *The Exorcist*. Rather than entering the film through Baldwin's critique, I want to reenter it now through his more capacious capacity to connect with unlikely bits of reality that other black queer viewers smuggle into these films.

If Davis teaches Baldwin to "find a way to use [his] strangeness," then the devil too might have its otherworlding uses. With her deadwhite greenish pallor, her disastrous lips, and her wickedly tensed and intelligent forehead, Regan exists as the unchosen shadow of Baldwin's investments in Davis. He may not be open to her, but other black queer audiences are. In that spirit, I now turn to passing references to *The Exorcist* hinted at in the fictions of James Earl Hardy, Larry Duplechan, and G. Winston James. Each representation unlocks a vexed identification with possession that revolves around a felt tension between agency and passivity, self and other, and, finally, pleasure and trauma as they take hold within the erotic life.

Black Queers Do *The Exorcist*

In the first half of this article, I have argued that black horror fans are too often cast as being traumatically beholden to some greater real that takes precedence over the generic thrills of the horror genre. Pushing back against dominant and sometimes totalizing accounts of black reception, I turn now to fictional works that allow me to configure a different relationship between black viewers and mainstream horror. Such representations multiply black viewing practices. They offer alternatives to the standing assumptions that black horror fans are predominantly (1) attracted to the genre as a way of working through more pressing racial traumas; (2) fixating on some allegedly more horrifying reality backgrounded within these films rather than their more thrilling paranormal foreground; (3) largely moved and triggered by collective experiences shared equally by all black audiences rather than by those based more in their own uniquely formative experiences. In so doing, they push back against accounts that either too sweepingly reduce black life to horror or reduce black pleasure in horror to a cathartic way of working through traumas that they readily share with a larger black collective.

I now return to *The Exorcist* from the vantage point of black gay fiction so that I can part ways with Baldwin's reading and offer a new take on its meaning for black audiences. Although my texts depart from Baldwin's disinterest in the film, they align with his account of "smuggling" insofar as they disidentify with its white heroine to locate unlikely hints of black queer reality. In so doing, they smuggle black and queer viewings past Baldwin and back into a classical horror tradition that never had any interest in representing them.

The queer thrill that Andrew Scahill reads into *The Exorcist* nicely resonates with the brief allusions to the film that appear in Larry

Duplechan's novels *Eight Days a Week* (1985) and *Blackbird* (1986), James Earl Hardy's *B-Boy Blues* (1994), and G. Winston James's *Shaming the Devil* (2009). As Scahill notes, the queer "thrill" of watching Regan is based on the freedoms that possession affords its subject to "enact the transgressive desires" written out by normative selfhood.[28] These black gay protagonists thus take Regan as an apt figure for their own no less vexed embodiment. As Regan, they are besieged by excessive desires that alienate them from their accustomed selves (even as they seem to articulate pleasures that they may have repressed in normative selfhood). Coincidentally, all references to possession appear in contexts when black gay men experience an attraction to their ultimate erotic ideals: hypermasculine, highly racialized men who hope to possess, dominate, and even harm them. The shattering states that they experience often muddle any clear demarcations between erotic agency and passivity. Through close readings of these moments alongside the film, I locate black spectators more capaciously—and more queerly—within the horror genre in ways that have not yet become available in black horror studies. In such cases, the horror film does not unlock any easily collectivized feeling of racial trauma. Instead, dwelling on possession offers a far campier embrace of both the paranormal and the paranormative.

In James Earl Hardy's *B-Boy Blues*, the narrator uses *The Exorcist* to describe the rapture that he experiences while having sex with the ultimate "homie-sexual": the b-boy.[29] Getting with a b-boy, he hopes, will free him from his sexual inhibitions and "bring out the freak in me" (*BB*, 39). On the one hand, bringing out the freak is an act of self-possession that allows him to expand his erotic subjectivity. On the other, it is an act of possession. He can bring out the inner freak only by giving in to the other—the b-boy—who helps him give in to that lewd other locked up within himself. He activates this otherness with the titular b-boy, Raheim, who praises him for being "so fuckin' wicked" in the bedroom (*BB*, 63). This pleasure of giving in to what is freakish and wicked marks the beginnings of possession as Scahill describes it. From here on the subject of possession experiences himself not as a subject but as coming under the sway of an unrecognizably lewd other. In the climactic moment I examine below, the narrator turns to *The Exorcist* to articulate this rapture of letting go of his accustomed identity to come under the possession of another.

He thus appropriates the key tropes of possession—the speaking in tongues, the banging bed, the rolling eyes—to perform a pleasure that takes him beyond himself:

> "Oh yea, Bay-bee . . . ya wan' me ta take it, hunh?"
>
> *"Take it, Raheim, take it, yeah!"*
>
> "Ha, don' worry, cuz I'm gon' take it . . . ya jus' gotta give it up . . . now, give dat shit *up!*"
>
> I did.
>
> The scene was reminiscent of *The Exorcist*. Our faces were distorted, our eyes retreating to the backs of our heads. Our words were unintelligible, our hollering horrifying. Our breathing was so hot it was like fire. The headboard of the bed was drumming its own beat on the wall. The lamp on the dresser next to the bed fell to the floor. I could feel my blood pumping through me like raging waters out of control. I saw that his was, too; his veins were bulging through his skin. My body was twisting as if I were possessed. I clawed his back, digging my nails into his skin. Uh-huh, I was Linda Blair. (*BB*, 63)

In possession films, we know that the subject is possessed because they can speak in other tongues, usually Latin. Here too both men's speech becomes "unintelligible," as when Raheim climaxes just before this scene while "screaming something that sounded like Pig Latin" (*BB*, 60). Their hollering is "horrifying" because it playfully shocks them with hitherto repressed versions of themselves and one another. To be fucking wicked is thus to let go of oneself, one's humanity and attendant inhibitions, to experience a rapture that momentarily dissolves—or shatters—one's accustomed sense of sovereignty. In a twist on Muñoz's reading of Baldwin, Regan—with her "freakish beauty"—offers the narrator "something both liberatory and horrible": a way to "use my strangeness" in the bedroom.[30]

But how much of this performance is passive and how much agentive? The allusion to *The Exorcist* complicates how we locate the subject in this instance because it mixes the passivity of being overcome with the agency of giving a commanding performance. Importantly, the narrator does not claim to be Regan; instead, he sees himself as the actress who plays her, Linda Blair. His split allusion thus casts him as both within the scene and masterfully without. In the role of the possessed child, he is pleasurably overcome with his passivity. In the role of the talented starlet, however, he can boast of his more commanding ability to play the role. Getting into character, he performs a rapturous feeling of self-loss that allows him to bring up the wicked inner freak. He becomes, in this sense, the scream queen: horror's hallowed version of the diva. What he therefore masters (as Blair) is his ability to lose control (as Regan). And while disidentifying with Regan allows him to get into the scene, disidentifying with Blair allows him to look back approvingly on his role.

We might contrast the acclaim Hardy's narrator wholly accords to Blair with yet another look at the film, this one from the narrator of Larry Duplechan's earlier novel, *Eight Days a Week* (1985). He gives the glory of this moment not to Blair but to the too long uncredited actress who vocally performs the possessed Regan: Mercedes McCambridge. McCambridge's masterful ability to both demonize and masculinize Regan is complicated.[31] She channels possession by drinking raw eggs and chain-smoking (to roughen her voice) and by breaking her sobriety to perform while drunk on whiskey. To intensify the strained quality to her voice, she is tied to a chair. In a 1998 interview, McCambridge recounts:

> It wasn't hard for me to imagine the rage. . . . I utilize the thickness, all of that stuff, for the voice of Lucifer. . . . I don't think they had to do this but they did: they tore up a sheet and put me in restraints with [sic] around my neck and my arms behind the chair and my knees and my feet so that I would feel like Linda Blair whom I've never met. While she was carrying on in the bed that [sic] I would be doing the same thing physically.[32]

Her methods blur the lines between the agency of acting and the helplessness of willingly being acted on by distorting substances. Her masterful presence is generated in part by her willingness to get drunk and actually embody a gasping experience of self-loss. The director applauds her ability to subject herself to all the "duress" she embodied to make the role real. In her 2011 interview, she admits that such restrained status is required to play at being possessed: "It has to happen when you have no freedom."[33] So, acting out her unfreedom backstage, she expertly performs possession in ways that further entangle the power struggle that Hardy's narrator witnesses during this scene. Counter to what he sees on-screen, it is not just that Regan is trapped inside the demon Pazuzu, but that the adult McCambridge is trapped inside the dissembling body of Linda Blair. Although Blair does do her own work—"Uh-huh"—she also takes credit for McCambridge's theatrics for years until McCambridge sues the studio for the right to appear in the credits.

As a "trivia receptacle and detail monger," Duplechan's narrator, Johnnie, recovers this credited diva to her rightful place, just as he does elsewhere with other black women singers (E, 240). He references McCambridge during a taxing musical tour. Overworked, he abandons his otherwise smooth demeanor and now "mumbled curses in a voice not unlike Mercedes McCambridge's voice-overs in *The Exorcist*."[34] Such an allusion lands queerly. It marks an alienating shift in Johnnie's demeanor by identifying his otherwise feminine singing voice—"Even *sings* like a girl"—with that of a woman who worked hard to play a mannish girl (E, 49). To this degree, it shows the behind-the-scenes strain of his labor as he drifts from his accustomed image of himself. In noting McCambridge's labor, he pays homage to her talent in his exhaustion. The joke lands not because the voice in his throat belongs to a female, but because it belongs to a female who—like him—could so masterfully play across the gender spectrum that she was mistaken for a male.

The reference also activates how exhausted Johnnie is not only from work but also from his domestic struggles with his domineering boyfriend, Keith, whom he adores for his whiteness. He "worshipped" Keith, as "my blond fetish incarnate": "I loved Keith's dick to the point of religion. I made up names for it like a primitive tribe might name its god over and over" (E, 171, 90, 192). Yet Keith's "overzealous possessiveness" makes him violent, and he demands that Johnnie give up his job to stay home (E, 195). Johnnie goes from skipping breakfast to balance his career with Keith—instead, "I gulped down three raw eggs"—to enduring violent tirades that curtail Johnnie's freedom (E, 128). Here McCambridge's furious mumblings do not relay—as with Hardy—an unintelligible rapture; instead, they signal the unfreedom that she endures to make art for a public who seems unlikely to remember her. By listening for McCambridge in Johnnie's voice, we hear many things at once: the gruff break in his otherwise smoothly feminine composure; the tragic foreshadowing that he will soon be upstaged by other performers; and, above all, the worn quality of his voice as he is overcome by someone who violently wishes to possess him.

Johnnie's relationship to *The Exorcist* gets a backstory in Duplechan's subsequent novel, *Blackbird* (1986): a prequel in which Johnnie comes out in high school. Watching the film in his small, conservative, largely white town, Johnnie feels exactly the kind of spiritual terror that Baldwin distances himself from. While one friend laughed as "Linda Blair spewing hot guacamole," and another puked, "only I seemed to have been moved to a profound sense of spiritual guilt" as a gay youth.[35] Feeling "a sudden fear of eternal damnation (or terrestrial demonic possession at the very least)," he confesses to his pastor (*B*, 150). By the next day he is "completely over the notion that my gayness is inherently evil," but the priest and Johnnie's family now regard his homosexuality as "possession by unclean spirits" (*B*, 150, 153). His baffled response—"Like in *The Exorcist?*"—casts him in the role of the actress, now reluctantly having to act out an affliction that he no longer believes in (*B*, 153). He may no longer wish "to be normal," but he is forced to undergo an exorcism and told exactly what to expect: "Spirits leave your body, they may come out as a sneeze or a coughing spell or something like that. I've had one or two people throw up" (*B*, 153, 160). To really play the part, as McCambridge knows, you must have no freedom, and Johnnie does this by giving the pastor and Johnnie's family all the pathos of a black queer boy forced to undergo an exorcism.

Camp is notably absent from his delivery and his recounting. It is a tool that he is aware of but whose strategy of ironic distancing remains unavailable to him and to us in this moment: "If it hadn't been me down there on [the exorcist] Solomon Hunt's living-room floor, I might have found a certain dark humor in the situation. But it *was* me. And it wasn't funny. I felt sad and cold, and very much alone. And I knew what I had to do" (*B*, 162). He screams. Hard. He refuses to "throw up for them," but everyone "assumed my unclean spirits departed my tortured little body in the scream" (*B*, 162). This aggrieved scream adds to Duplechan's earlier engagement with *The Exorcist*—and to Johnnie's passing McCambridge quip later in life—a longer, sadder queer complaint. The loneliness that he voices as a youth trapped in a small town compounds his later expression as an older singer who still feels trapped in his new city life. His worship of that punishing whiteness feels only like a second, more crushing form of possession. His vexed identification with *The Exorcist* persists, perhaps because he still experiences his erotic life as a black gay man through some degree of alienation and unfreedom. Though now openly gay, he seems no freer—no more self-possessed—in those moments when he gives in to his innermost desires.

Both of these black gay characters use *The Exorcist* to dramatize overwhelming feelings of estrangement and self-loss brought about by an erotic ideal. In the short story collection *Shaming the Devil* (2009), G. Winston James delivers a more difficult rendition of possession in his story "Somewhere Nearby." There his nameless cruising narrator is lured out into the woods by two thuggish black men he has been pursuing. Soon he realizes that they plan to kill him, and the remainder of the story is graphically located within the moments leading up to his own death. What makes the story so "haunting," as Darius Bost notes, is that the narrator comes to realize that some part of himself, though frightened, has always thrilled to become the object of another man's eroticized violence.[36] In the story's climactic moment, he secretly masturbates one of his two assailants (a man he calls Tupac) to wring one last bit of pleasure from an erotic life he still cannot understand. In what he terms an act of "self-affirmation and pseudo-heroic resignation," he practices the agency of surrender.[37] He surrenders not only to his imminent death but also to his vexed ability to somehow find pleasure in it. And at this moment we again find ourselves in *The Exorcist*.

The assailant, who is also aroused by the violence, allows himself to be masturbated on one condition: the dying narrator can never mention it to anyone. The narrator notes the absurdity of this moment as follows: "I can't say anything with a gag in my mouth, even if I tried . . . I cannot cause letters to rise on my skin like Regan in *The Exorcist*. I'm not altogether sure that Tupac would be able to read them even if I could" (*SD*, 111). This rash of letters refers to a key moment in the film that helps me draw together several allusions to possession that appear elsewhere in other short stories from the collection. The allusion references a moment when the once sweet Regan—now raunchily possessed—manages to halt her lewd antics long enough to send her mother a message through her sore-crusted body. Her mother unbuttons her nightie to find that the words *help me* have pitifully materialized across Regan's chest (see figs. 1 and 2). The devil perhaps allows Regan this supplication to tease the mother, Chris, with the suffering, submerged presence of her once sweet child. But the meaning this phrase takes within the short story itself is far more slippery. To see why, we first need to look back at the film itself.

In the film, right before the words *help me* surface on Regan's stomach, a detective reviews Regan's case with Chris while staring at a picture of Little Red Riding Hood. As Scahill notes, this quick glance signifies that "Regan seems to exist quite literally inside the Wolf's belly. . . . The beast has swallowed her whole and suppressed her soul into its belly, awaiting the Woodsman to release her from consumption."[38] There is no straightforward way to apply this allusion in our reading of the story, however, for James's cruisers all celebrate their sexual conquests in just such predatory language. They can so adeptly cruise one another, they boast, because they too are "so attuned, like wolves" (*SD*, 57). It is not that the narrator is simply asking to be saved from his bashers, then: he is also asking to be saved from his own willfully erotic body. He seems as much at the mercy of his own impulses as of those of the men who beat him. The beast that "has swallowed [him] whole and suppressed [his] soul"—to borrow Scahill's phrase—is a figuration of his own alienating sex drive. Like Regan, he seems possessed, yearning to cry out from within himself. He is done in by his own desires. He is undone by them. They permit him no feelings of self-possession, so he allows us to read this unlettered phrase—*help me*—as if it were a deep-down plea from the innocent child that he once was. Having laid out his formative traumas, he seems to beg the reader to free him from his own compulsive body.

Possession thus concentrates the feeling of being trapped within a lewd and unwilled body. But unlike Regan, the narrator is not so easily the passive victim of possession. Instead, he embraces his desires, mixing agency and passivity. As Darius Bost argues of the

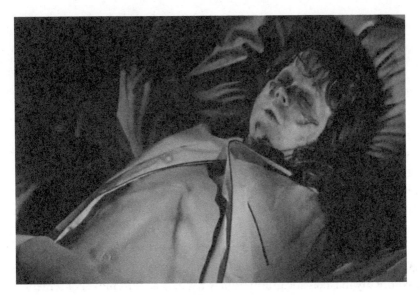

Fig. 1. Image of the possessed and badly scarred Regan, with the words *help me* beginning to form across her sunken stomach.

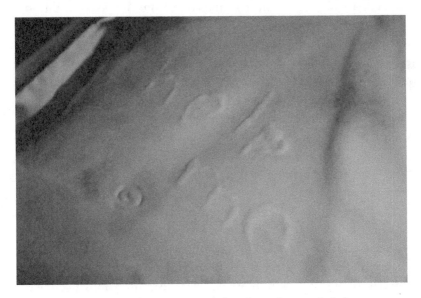

Fig. 2. A close-up of Regan's stomach, where the words *help me* appear more clearly now in the form of keloid scars.

story, "Acknowledging that his incessant desire will position him outside of innocent victimhood, the corpse still demands the pleasure promised from these men as potential sexual partners, even now, as his murders. The victim refuses to sanitize the messiness of black queerness produced in these tangles of death and desire."[39] Indeed, he may feel trapped within his erotic body by virtue of these formative traumas, but he still claims its vexed pleasures in ways that signal self-possession: "I am still driven by the erotic, and I am grateful" (SD, 112). He is possessed insofar as he is controlled by alienating drives, yet he is self-possessing insofar as he can finally claim them in a life-affirming way. He looks back on his erotic life in a cinematic way, as if he were, not unlike Linda Blair, the star of a sexualized desecration: "I realize I have been training myself for this moment of desecration. Unfortunately this night of torment has come well before my masochistic graduation. Cast in this snuff film . . . I remember things in this moment that were long forgotten, but explain so much about how I came, almost unbeknownst to me, to link sex and violence" (SD, 110). Using carefully placed commas, James breaks this phrase—"how I came, almost unbeknownst to me"— to suggest that the narrator is alienated from the very conditions that allow him to attain his orgasm. The reason he comes remains opaque—"unbeknownst to me"—yet it is these very conditions that bring him a vexed pleasure that he tries his best to embrace. He thus casts himself as being both the desiring subject and the yielding object of this transaction. In light of his experiences, he seems himself as having auditioned for a role that he neither fully chooses nor understands but still tries to perform in a convincing way.

The word *desecration*, moreover, powerfully frames what the three men—the narrator as well as the other two—are doing with his body as sacrilegious. These violent sexual acts register as blasphemous in ways that once more help activate his following allusion to *The Exorcist*. Father Karras describes "satanism—meaning people who can't have any sexual pleasure unless it's connected to a blasphemous action."[40] In the film, this is signified by a makeshift cock and pair of breasts—both bloody—that are grafted onto a statue of the Virgin Mary. In the novel, it is also signified by a vandalized Bible that describes "an imagined homosexual encounter involving

Mary Magdalene and the Blessed Virgin Mary" (*TE*, 96). The possessed were subject to acts that spectacularly link sex, violence, and queerness in blasphemous acts. The possessed were, Blatty writes, "helpless in the state of possession, they had regularly attended Satanic orgies at which they had varied their erotic fare: Mondays and Tuesdays, heterosexual copulation; Thursdays, sodomy, fellatio and cunnilingus with homosexual partners" (*TE*, 241). Such desecration interarticulates demonic sex with queer group sex performed in honor of the emphatically phallic god that possesses Regan: Pazuzu. Pazuzu is fashioned with a "bulbous, jutting, stubby penis" and "a feral grin" (*TE*, 5). He exemplifies exactly the violent and phallic forms of masculinity that the men of "Somewhere Nearby" perform in their violent desires for one another.

It is difficult, though, to say whether or not James wishes to exorcise this kind of erotic bedevilment or to embrace queer expressions that are marked as demonic. Turning to the devil is useful in that it allows him to embrace desires elsewhere regarded as shameful. Rather than follow this scene further, I will demonstrate this ambivalence by turning to one final scene from another story in the collection that further complicates how we understand possession. This moment does not reference *The Exorcist*, but it deploys the word *pig* in ways that powerfully activate its place at the intersections of gay and religious histories. The wolf—the aggressive male top—is but one model of gay virility; the pig is another. As Tim Dean notes, barebacking cultures were giving new prominence to these desires as "wolves metamorphosed into pigs": "Being a pig entails committing oneself to sexual excess, to pushing beyond boundaries of propriety and corporeal integrity; being a pig thus positions a man for membership in a sexual avant-garde."[41] In James's story "Path," the narrator's claim to the category of "the pig" both activates this commitment and questions its volitional status as a fully agentive or empowering act. His narrator is late to work because he stops to have sex with a stranger in a subway stall. While doing so, he sees a homeless man watching them through the crack with a "lunatic eye" (*SD*, 59). Rather than feeling shame, the narrator is delighted: "Recognizing how much of a freak he was, the pig in me almost swooned" (*SD*, 59). Only in the most straightforward sense can we take the narrator to be the heroic pig that Dean describes:

a no-limits man who gets off on voyeurism. To see why, we must cut to the biblical allusion on our way back into *The Exorcist*.

In the Gospel according to Matthew, Jesus exorcises a demon from a possessed man by casting it out into a nearby group of pigs, which immediately drown themselves. Throughout *The Exorcist* the devil several times mocks this moment by referring to Regan as his "pig." He often does this when he invites others to desecrate Regan. In the most infamous scene, the possessed Regan—having just masturbated with a bloody crucifix—forces her mother's face between her legs, demanding that she lick. In the novel, Regan moans just before this moment—"Aahhh, little pig mother!"—and concludes by "sensually" sliding the cross back in while crooning over her own body, "Ahh, there's my sow, yes, my sweet honey piglet" (*TE*, 205). By calling Regan his pig, he declares his sexualized dominion over her. "The sow is mine!"—he shouts to a group of doctors in the film, right before demanding that they fuck her (*SD*, 114). Being the devil's pig thus entails surrendering your body to others. Much of the film suggests that Regan herself is not present during these moments. But scholars counter that she is both present enough to spell *help me* and aware enough to gratefully kiss a pastor once she is exorcised, as if she could dimly remember how good the church was to her. What makes us unsure whether or not she was conscious for these actions is how often she swoons during these early acts, as if the knowledge of her actions were too unbearable.

Returning, then, to that line from James—"the pig in me almost swooned"—we see now that the phrase is cut with an ambivalence that is legible only when we read intertextually. Because the devil calls his helpless vessel his "piglet," it is possible that the narrator is alluding to some truer and more reserved self that is held captive within his erotic body. The pig is no longer simply, as it was with Dean, an innermost self, hungry for unlimited intimacies. We can only meet it with questions. Does the pig in me swoon inside because it is overcome with shock and disgust at my outward actions? Does it swoon joyously—*perversely*—at its unimaginable luck? Or is it some combination of the two? Does the pig in me—no longer held captive by my reserve—rejoice to see that I have finally let go of my shame and given in to what I most want deep down? That I have finally given free rein to what others would call my inner demons? All readings are in fact necessary if we are to experience what the erotics of possession makes possible for James. In possession, the subject—also a nonsubject—performs desires that force into crisis the very ideas he has of himself. In the throes of passion, he performs acts that later make him feel conflicted. Such a pig might—when he comes down—swoon not from joy but in the way that Regan does. He might swoon from his inability to endure such acts that he cannot bear to see himself performing.

Throughout his stories James thus deploys possession in ways that never allow us to simply equate exorcism with a desired freedom. We witness the various efforts of therapists, priests, friends, and parents to converge on the bodies of black queers to force them to renounce their pleasures. Sometimes exorcism articulates a yearning to find freedom from self-destructive behaviors, and in other instances it allegorizes a conversion therapy that is forced on black gay men. While it is certainly possible, then, to read *help me* as the traumatized black queer once more seeking help from "white science" to escape these self-destructive impulses, it is equally possible to imagine the call as coming from elsewhere. Given how the narrator leans into this pleasure, the plea *help me* might be, in fact, a strained call from the misunderstood pig in him who still hopes to be let out. It might be yet another iteration of the voice that opens the story collection—a queer boy who cannot understand his attraction to his uncle's nude body, and whose yearning falls back on a strange plea: "Please, please . . . Satan" (*SD*, 15). The answer to who he is seems to lie not with God but with the devil, and in this way he is little different from how James remembers himself as a queer boy, puzzled by his erections: "In my pre-teens, fascinated with demons and black magic, I attempted on several occasions to summon not just any demon, but Satan himself. I wanted to talk with Lucifer about God since my prayers had always seemed to go unanswered."[42] Turning from God seems to draw us back into the same curious question that possession poses: What might I want when I let go of who I thought I was?

Keeping alive this vexed state of possession, I prefer that we leave all potential readings in play when attempting to analyze what *The*

Exorcist means for black, queer, and feminist viewers. Indeed, only by dwelling in this place of irresolution and inner conflict can we understand the intimate place that possession has in the erotic world of James's fiction. The conflicted black queer subject both does and doesn't beg for release from the overwhelming desires of his erotic body. He both does and doesn't delight in wolfing down and pigging out on gruff strangers. He is both the wickedly subversive figure that some feminist and queer scholars take Regan to be and, at the same time, the helpless subject cruelly driven by an alien force that has dominion over him. He is, I mean, everywhere just as vexed, complicated, and messy as our identifications with *The Exorcist* itself.

....

BRANDON S. CALLENDER is assistant professor of English literature at Brandeis University, where he specializes in black queer and black horror studies. He is completing a manuscript on black queer men's intimacies and belongings, tentatively titled *The Charge of the Other in Black Gay Men's Literatures*.

Acknowledgments

I am grateful to my colleagues Caren Irr and Paul Morrison for workshopping an earlier version of this draft, and to Naima Karczmar, Mehak Khan, Kyra Sutton, and the rest of the editorial board of *Qui Parle* for their insightful suggestions and revisions.

Notes

1. When the black gay author Samuel R. Delany refuses to capitalize *black* in 1999, he does so as a reminder that the lowercase term once held a unique political and affective importance for his generation that is now hastily being abandoned. I am struck by how many other contemporary black queer writers, like myself, express feeling at home in now outmoded terms for blackness—colored, Negro, negr*ess*—that complicate its status as a universally shared language. If I continue to inhabit the lowercase, it is out of not just custom and comfort but the joy of seeing blackness expressed, polyphonically, in all its complexity. See Delany, "Racism and Science Fiction."
2. Brooks, *Searching for Sycorax*, 9.

3. Williams, building on work of James B. Twitchell.

4. Coleman, *Horror Noire*, xvii.

5. Muñoz, *Disidentifications*, 12.

6. See Twitchell, *Dreadful Pleasures*; Carroll, *Philosophy of Horror*; and Hantke, introduction.

7. Imarisha, *Sycorax's Daughters*, xv. I am alluding to James B. Twitchell's monograph *Dreadful Pleasures: An Anatomy of Modern Horror* (1985).

8. Taylor, *Darkly*, 10.

9. LaValle, *Ballad of Black Tom*, 143. See also Ruff, *Lovecraft Country*.

10. Due, *Good House*, 194.

11. Carroll, *Philosophy of Horror*, 65.

12. Baldwin, *The Devil Finds Work*, 121 (hereafter cited as *DFW*).

13. Clover, *Men, Women, and Chainsaws*, 67.

14. Hart, *Monstrous Forms*, 22.

15. Rockoff, *Horror of It All*, 125.

16. Friedkin, *The Exorcist*.

17. Marks, "Star of the Morning."

18. Wood, "Return of the Repressed," 59.

19. Wood, "Return of the Repressed," 62.

20. Wood, "Return of the Repressed," 62.

21. Scahill, *Revolting Child*, 22.

22. Rockoff, *Horror of It All*, 127. In his 2019 tome of black joy, *The Book of Delights*, the poet Ross Gay offers a similarly campy experience of rewatching *The Exorcist* in a theater. The very scenes that once terrified him as a child are now made joyful by the irreverence of his surrounding audience: "When Linda Blair peed on the rug this time someone said to the screen, 'Oh no she didn't!' And when her head spun around, someone yelled, 'That girl is trippin'!' At which point I realized this movie, which had occupied for years a grave space in my imagination, was actually silly. I was freed from the grave. Or rather, I was offered another version of the grave—laughter in its midst" (239–40).

23. Gillespie, *Film Blackness*, 11.

24. Muñoz, *Disidentifications*, 15.

25. Muñoz, *Disidentifications*, 18.

26. Sedgwick, "Queer and Now," 4.

27. Sedgwick, "Queer and Now," 3.

28. Scahill, *Revolting Child*, 77.

29. Hardy, *B-Boy Blues*, 28 (hereafter cited as *BB*).

30. Munoz, *Disidentifications*, 18.
31. Olson and Reinhard point out that "McCambridge frequently played butch characters," queering the nature of Regan's possessed persona (*Possessed Women, Haunted States*, 27).
32. Kermode, *Fear of God*.
33. Shields, "One Hell of a Performance."
34. Duplechan, *Eight Days a Week*, 220 (hereafter cited as *E*).
35. Duplechan, *Blackbird*, 149–50 (hereafter cited as *B*).
36. Bost, "In the Life," 159.
37. James, *Shaming the Devil*, 111 (hereafter cited as *SD*).
38. Scahill, *Revolting Child*, 66.
39. Bost, "Queering Violence," 198.
40. Blatty, *The Exorcist*, 166 (hereafter cited as *TE*).
41. Dean, *Unlimited Intimacy*, 49. Compare this with Barbara Creed's embrace of Regan as a subject "who refuses to take up her proper place in the symbolic order" and convenes "a return of the unclean, untrained, unsymbolized body . . . constructed as a rebellion of filthy, lustful, carnal, female flesh" (*Monstrous-Feminine*, 38). Or Scahill's queer delight at watching Regan unleash "*rage*—queer rage—tingled with blood, with shit, with cum, with pus, with vomit, with disease, with every other bodily abjection that the social order links to queerness turned on its oppressors, saturating them in the disgusting volition of its own displaced aggression" (*Revolting Child*, 61).
42. James, "Simple Truth," 190.

References

Baldwin, James. *The Devil Finds Work*. New York: First Vintage International, 2011.

Blatty, William Peter. *The Exorcist*. New York: HarperCollins, 2011.

Bost, Darius. "Queering Violence in the Stories of G. Winston James." In *Black Sexual Economies: Race and Sex in a Culture of Capital*, edited by Adrienne D. Davis and BSE Collective, 187–99. Champaign: University of Illinois Press, 2019.

Brooks, Kinitra D. *Searching for Sycorax: Black Women's Hauntings of Contemporary Horror*. New Brunswick, NJ: Rutgers University Press, 2018.

Carroll, Noël. *The Philosophy of Horror; or, Paradoxes of the Heart*. New York: Routledge, 1990.

Clover, Carol J. *Men, Women, and Chainsaws: Gender in the Modern Horror Film*. Princeton, NJ: Princeton University Press, 2015.

Coleman, Robin R. Means. *Horror Noire: Blacks in American Horror Films from the 1890s to Present*. New York: Routledge, 2011.

Creed, Barbara. *The Monstrous-Feminine: Film, Feminism, Psychoanalysis*. New York: Routledge, 1993.

Dean, Tim. *Unlimited Intimacy: Reflections on the Subculture of Bareback*. Chicago: University of Chicago Press, 2009.

Delany, Samuel R. "Racism and Science Fiction." In *Dark Matter: A Century of Speculative Fiction from the African Diaspora*, edited by Sheree R.Thomas, 383–97. New York: Warner Books, 2000.

Due, Tananarive. *The Good House*. New York: Washington Square, 2003.

Duplechan, Larry. *Blackbird*. New York: St. Martin's, 1986.

Duplechan, Larry. *Eight Days a Week*. Boston: Alyson, 1985.

Friedkin, William, dir. *The Exorcist*. Warner Brothers, 1973.

Gay, Ross. *The Book of Delights*. Chapel Hill, NC: Algonquin Books of Chapel Hill, 2019.

Gillespie, Michael Boyce. *Film Blackness: American Cinema and the Idea of Black Film*. Durham, NC: Duke University Press, 2016.

Hantke, Steffen. Introduction to *Horror Film: Creating and Marketing Fear*, edited by Steffen Hantke, vii–xiii. Jackson: University Press of Mississippi, 2004.

Hardy, James Earl. *B-Boy Blues: A Seriously Sexy, Fiercely Funny, Black-on-Black Love Story*. Los Angeles: Alyson, 1994.

Hart, Adam Charles. *Monstrous Forms: Moving Image Horror across Media*. New York: Oxford University Press, 2020.

Imarisha, Walidah. Preface to *Sycorax's Daughters*, edited by Kinitra Brooks, Linda D. Addison, and Susana Morris, xii–xvi. San Francisco: Cedar Grove, 2017.

James, G. Winston. *Shaming the Devil*. Hollywood, CA: Top Pen, 2009.

James, G. Winston. "The Simple Truth." In *Spirited: Awakening the Soul and Black Gay/Lesbian Identity*, edited by G. Winston James and Lisa C. Moore, 189–97. New Orleans, LA: RedBone Press, 2006.

Kermode, Mark. *The Fear of God: Twenty-Five Years of "The Exorcist."* London: British Broadcasting Corporation, 1998.

LaValle, Victor. *The Ballad of Black Tom*. New York: Tom Doherty Associates, 2016.

Marks, Laura, writer. "Star of the Morning." *The Exorcist*, season 1, episode 6, directed by Jennifer Phang. Chicago Fox, 2016.

Muñoz, José Esteban. *Disidentifications: Queers of Color and the Performance of Politics*. Minneapolis: University of Minnesota Press, 2014.

Olson, Christopher J., and CarrieLynn D. Reinhard. *Possessed Women, Haunted States: Cultural Tensions in Exorcism Cinema*. London: Lexington, 2016.

Rockoff, Adam. *The Horror of It All: One Moviegoer's Love Affair with Masked Maniacs, Frightened Virgins, and the Living Dead*. New York: Scribner, 2015.

Ruff, Matt. *Lovecraft Country*. New York: HarperCollins, 2016.

Scahill, Andrew. *The Revolting Child in Horror Cinema: Youth, Rebellion, and Queer Spectatorship*. New York: Palgrave Macmillan, 2015.

Sedgwick, Eve Kosofsky. "Queer and Now." In *Tendencies*, 1–22. Durham, NC: Duke University Press, 1993.

Shields, Meg. "One Hell of a Performance: How Mercedes McCambridge Gave a Demon a Voice." Film School Rejects, May 8, 2020. filmschool rejects.com/mercedes-mccambridge-the-exorcist.

Taylor, Leila. *Darkly: Black History and America's Gothic Soul*. New York: Repeater, 2019.

Twitchell, James B. *Dreadful Pleasures: An Anatomy of Modern Horror*. New York: Oxford University Press, 1985.

Wester, Maisha L. *African American Gothic: Screams from Shadowed Places*. New York: Palgrave Macmillan, 2012.

Wood, Robin. "Return of the Repressed." In *Robin Wood on the Horror Film: Collected Essays and Reviews*, edited by Barry Keith Grant, 57–62. Detroit: Wayne State University Press, 2018.

Poems by Oksana Vasyakina
and Elena Kostyleva

TRANSLATED BY HELENA KERNAN

Oksana Vasyakina and Elena Kostyleva are contemporary Russian poetesses who contribute to Ф-письмо (F Letter), a digital platform that publishes, critiques, and celebrates feminist writing.[1] Their work is testament to a generational change in Russophone poetry, which has seen a decline in the certainties and declamatory style of the previous generation in favor of all-embracing polyphony and linguistic experimentation, an ethical commitment to decolonization and leftist politics, and a strong focus on diverse spectrums of gender and sexuality.

Vasyakina's "Girl" is the latest in a series of poems that trace the trials, tribulations, joys, and hopes of the author's own biography. The poem was published not long after her debut novel, *Рана* (*Wound*), a hybrid text that includes essays, poems, and novelistic plot devices and enters into dialogue with several female thinkers, both past and present. Staged as an intimate conversation between lesbian partners, "Girl" imagines two women having a biological baby together: the physical sensations of extracting spinal cells, implanting an embryo,

QUI PARLE   Vol. 31, No. 1, June 2022
DOI 10.1215/10418385-9669503   © 2022 Editorial Board, *Qui Parle*

and sensing the life force of a partner inside the womb. The fabric of the verse delights in the feelings of closeness and warmth that emanate from both the act of communication and the displacement of normative conceptions of reproduction and the creation of life. "We live an ordinary life," the poem begins, in a powerful reframing of the limits of the ordinary. Vasyakina's biological vision is renewed, expanded, and liberated from any association with the male.

Kostyleva, in her poem "Morning," constructs a Freudian riff on the implications of contemporary porn for ethics and conceptions of humanity, focusing on Pornhub as the locus of fantasy, timelessness, storytelling, and psychic transformation. The work intersects with the paranormative at the borders of what is ordinarily considered human, as the figures in the verse vacillate between incarnations of people and flamboyant, folkloric/nightmarish creatures. Kostyleva's interweaving of psychoanalysis and philosophy in this poem echoes much of her previous work, which is influenced by her own practice as a psychoanalyst. Here, dissociation, loneliness, perversion, and desire fuse together, making the poem as much about the human psyche as it is about the body and its capabilities and constraints.

Girl

we live an ordinary life
the blisters on your toe sting
and i repeat after you: yes it hurts, yes it's unbearable,
    it will stop soon hang on
i touch your dark curly head
and my hand grows into a huge maternal hand
i bring you a basin of icy water so you can soak the
    soles of your feet
and i stand there, hands on hips, waiting for the pain to
    subside at least a little
i want to engulf you whole like a serene ship and carry
    you through the pain
i want to engulf everything that's alive here
become a mother to all living things

i'm growing bigger and the membrane of my body
     shivers, before long i will become this world

i know your warmth i know how your body fills
     everything in the space of the room with
     meaning
there's a bond between us
slow invisible tentacles caress each other and gleam in
     the darkness
and pierce my stomach they stroke everything inside,
     unrelenting
i feel you inside my cheek, my thigh
you pierce inside me
your dry scent your skin murmurs beneath my hand
you smell like straw, tar, and bark
i know what your head smells like
and the scent of your mouth too
i know you

i like to press my whole face into your soft stomach
and lie like that, feeling you undeniably alive
you're alive and everything inside you is relentlessly
     alive

my friend is carrying a baby inside her i see how her
     body has changed
she's becoming a full-grown, ripening woman she's
     maturing like an elongated pear
and we speak about the baby
about our little girl, mine and yours,
she'll look like me because i'm going to carry her
but if you give me your egg cell
i can carry you inside myself
our girl will drink milk from my breast and grow inside
     me
i'll feed her with my body and my warmth

you'll be there

when the sharp needle implants the seed in the wall of
    my uterus
and i feel the pain

i'll be there
when they take out your egg cells
and you feel the pain

somewhere far away there's an experimental lab
where scientists have discovered how to extract the raw
    material for conception from women's spinal
    cords
you can take some stem cells, then, after a long
    procedure where you insert the mitochondria,
    you inject them into the egg cell
then, they say, two women will be able to have a baby
and it has to be a little girl because in a female set of
    chromosomes there's no Y-chromosome
a little girl who will be me and you but different
our number three
but for now it's just an experiment
they say yes one day in fifty years or so it will be
    possible
i've never tried it but i know that taking cells from the
    spine is unbearably painful
maybe they'll figure out how to make it painless

i close my eyes and imagine
a girl with your coarse, wiry hair
your radiant olive skin and dark brown eyes, pupils
    blurred into irises
there's something elusive and mine in the girl
i recognize her
i'm longing for her
and she's here somewhere between us, the walls already
    echo her voice
and her warmth beats against my chest, i can feel it

I often think about what Freud would have written if he'd visited a contemporary porn site. I also think about what humanity might tell itself if it took the trouble to describe it all. [Kostyleva's epigraph]

Morning

The man-knight fucks the woman-bird
She's only woman down below, her plumage
is lush black feathers—they hide her face
("Either a bird or a cat or a dame is mine")
(there was only one song
in prehistoric times)

The essay by contemporary philosopher Nick Land,
"A Quick-and-Dirty Introduction to Accelerationism,"
Begins by saying that we're too late
That we're too slow for
Too slow, fuck, the time for contemplation is over
Such a shame

Will I manage to die?
Everyone else has managed somehow—that calms me

A dull, mechanical spider-monster, diligent as a
     lawnmower
I stopped watching

Beast, a real-life succubus with canine paws,
that split at the groin into two round, woolly muscles
Monstrosity—and the girl, all white, her breasts
     dazzling white
Blue eyes, an Esenin birch
Just like fucking Gianni Rodari

His member is like a big, stretched-out strawberry
(berry berry)
very like Nick Land, very Veronika Dolina

At the end of the first act of the great theater of fantasies
     pornhub

Dot com
He licks up her saliva with his tongue
Big as a spade
He finished inside her at one point
But there's no time on pornhub
Pornhub is liberated time

After that the monster releases a small, carnivorous fish
    into her
A lively, darting fish
And our blue-eyed
Girlie
Will be nothing but a puddle
Of luminous liquid of the sacred energy of life

And finally, the Wolf fucks the Fox (it's a cartoon)
Everything human
Finishes

At the same time
All the other trends are evolving
Described porn is becoming popular
Some people want to know
Who the characters are, what their jobs are, how it even
    happened
That they started fucking
Right there in the office
Who needs whom as who
Who's the boss lady
Who's the Master, who's the Slave
Who's lusting, who's doing the work

There's been a "ladies' section" for ages now
It's the same as the men's
The same huge cocks, brazen breasts
But slower
Women ask for it slower
—or harder!

The gap between the animal and the beast is growing
Some must be protected
(The sacred
Animals
Of modernity—
That's
All
Animals)
We must protect against others (as best we can, of
    course)
Denying our desire
In the throes of free multiple orgasms
In the unstoppable revolution of life

And the most essential thing is
You can't watch porn with real actors anymore
Or with animals or children—but who in their right
    mind would watch that abuse
It's tough for the detectives

But
Sketched in secret Japanese labs
With voice-overs added in Russia
Animated in China—
Everything is possible
You hear, everything

    . . . it's tough for the detectives
and the scholars
tough and unbearable

Anthropologists
Prefer not to see
Poets
Stay silent about the important things
Psychoanalysts
Know but are bound by a vow of silence

It's tough for the detectives
It penetrated my tongue

A conviction about what's human
—Well, is it tough for you, Major Tomin?
—Oh, it's so tough, Lena

those poor
Sherlock Holmeses
of my poor
childhood

Hey, does anyone remember Major Tomin?
You'll look back—but no one will be there

The psychoanalyst
And the wolf have died
The fox has died

The light is fading in the petting zoo
And it turns out that your entire identity
Your entire cherished agency
Never existed
Only a dissociative fugue
That's it,
You can choose
A new place to live
A new name
A new Petersburg text

One philosopher-boy
From somewhere far away
Like all philosophers,
Recounted
How his neighbor in this unfathomable city
During a normal conversation
Suddenly said he wanted a great love affair
Then died two months later

Lively, darting postcoital yearning,
The little empress fish
Ate up his insides

He couldn't even clean his house
Throw away all that
Degrading crap

How
can you counter that
How strong
Should these mechanisms be
What kind of protracted experience
Should they offer
How tightly
Should it be woven into everything else
So that not a single (lousy) dissociative fugue
Washes away the memory of you

....

HELENA KERNAN is a writer, translator, and researcher based in Berlin. She holds MA degrees in Slavic studies from the University of Cambridge and the University of California, Berkeley, and has spent time in Moscow, Saint Petersburg, Kyiv, and Perm working on projects related to contemporary art, documentary theater, historical memory, and human rights. As a translator, she focuses on contemporary Russophone poetry, twentieth-century Ukrainian texts, and the Russian avant-garde. In 2020 she was chosen as the inaugural translator of Contemporary Russian Poetry in Residence by Pushkin House.

Note

1. The identity of the "poetess" is key to the literary practice and political stance of the F Letter collective. It signals the reclaiming of a term that has historically been used to demean women writers and a reveling in the feminist potential of poetry.

The Prion as Nature's Undead

KATHLEEN POWERS

As a diagnostician, you like to think about how things become seen. The prion diseases appear as a ribbon, a trimming of the cortex in a diffusion-weighted MRI of the brain.[1] The tell is the bright white. Appearing as if an adhesive to the curves of the gray matter, the hyperintensity denotes the death of somae, the cell bodies of neurons.[2] This diagnostic sign, termed "ribboning," appears when "there are holes, like a sponge, in the brain itself" (fig. 1).[3] And if the brain is responding to the onslaught against it, it is not clear. Around the perforated tissue, there is no evidence of inflammation, no evidence of the body's recognition of infection, and no evidence of an immune response.[4] The hole, illegible, is less wound than abyss. It is what thought vanishes into.

The prion is a protein that infects the central nervous system. Unlike a virus particle or bacterium, the prion reproduces on the basis of its sheet-dense molecular architecture, in a reproduction reaction that occurs without the presence of DNA.[5] In this essay I apply Georges Canguilhem's criterion for life, biological normativity, to the prion to argue that the existence of the prion within living systems requires attention to how biological matter uses space, which,

QUI PARLE   Vol. 31, No. 1, June 2022
DOI 10.1215/10418385-9669514   © 2022 Editorial Board, *Qui Parle*

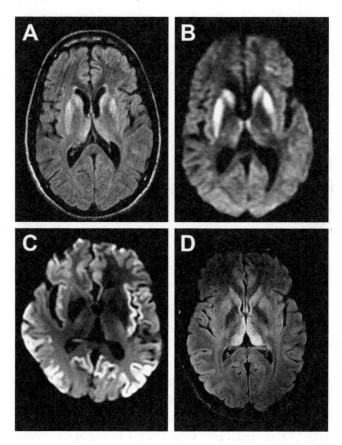

Fig. 1. Diagnostic signs in prion disease. Cortical ribboning in (C). A, B, and D demonstrate additional signs from the basal ganglia (A, B) and pulvinar nuclei (D) of prion infection. Mead and Rudge, "CJD Mimics and Chameleons," 116.

in the case of the prion, is its misfolding of other proteins. This essay is less invested in the similar question asked of viruses—are they alive?[6]—and is more invested in the analysis of how twentieth-century vitalism might account for biological agents that do not satisfy criteria for biological life. I argue that Canguilhem's biological normativity is a spatial phenomenon, a theory of life grounded in teratology and the history of disordered forms. Accordingly, I approach the agents of microscopic biology with attention to their formal quality. Building on work analyzing the legacy of twentieth-century vitalism and holism outside philosophy of medicine and biology[7] and on work that analyzes nature as space or architecture,[8] I apply Canguilhem's vitalist principles to space, allowing biomolecular structure, which for prions is the means of information propagation, to be analyzed as architecture. For if the prion's role is an analytic one—meaning, if there's something philosophy of biology can learn from the work of the prion about what exists—such learning follows from the prion's architectural role. The cause for writing is that the prion's use of space requires a philosophy of biology in which the role of molecular form is substituted for the role of genetic code.

The Prion

The prion perpetuates itself in a biology without language where the reproductive principle is not code but form. The prion *unfolds* and *folds*. The infectious prion protein, PrPSc (scrapie-associated prion protein), compresses the noninfectious protein, PrPC (cellular prion protein), between a series of unstable bonds until it has been copied (fig. 2; FAM, 11). The one requires the other: mice whose PrPC genes have been excised from their genome cannot be infected by PrPSc even if an infectious prion pathogen (PrPSc) is introduced, because these knockout mice[9] do not have the molecular substrate (PrPC) out of which the prion will create itself.[10]

That the cornerstone of the prion's virulence is its use of space makes my study of the prion's transposable structure an attempt at drug making. To understand the prion's architectural role is to elaborate a possibility for prion disease therapy and to consolidate the discipline of pharmacology as a science that addresses itself to form and dimension and not solely to code and a vectored line. All text has a direction that it presumes, requires. Medicine has used the directional requirements of the genetic code as linguistic text to generate therapies for severe diseases. For example, the purine and pyrimidine antimetabolites of chemotherapy, drugs like Cytarabine, allow a willful misspelling of genetic code, substituting a nonfunctional base look-alike into the line of DNA, a literary terminating

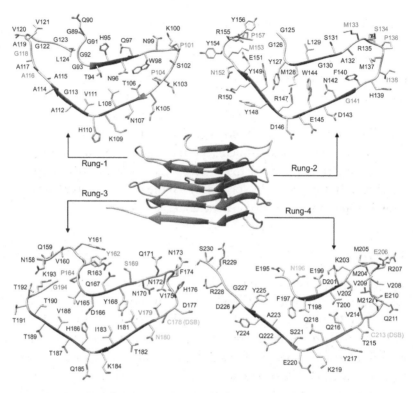

Fig. 2. The ladder-like, dynamic architecture of the PrPSc. Spagnolli et al., "Full Atomistic Model of Prion Structure and Conversion," 4.

chink as cancer cells undergo a process of replication. Cytarabine and similar treatments for cancer are effective. If you contract a prion disease, medicine has nothing for you.[11]

Prion diseases are called *spongiform* encephalopathies on account of what they do to the brain. For patients who have a prion disease, there are hallucinations:[12] rainbows;[13] a chair with no legs;[14] dead people;[15] a china cabinet, but at a slant;[16] men around a bed;[17] animals.[18] In such hallucinations, there seem to be two outward vectors: one, the attempt to maintain neurological function around the holes into which neural charge dissipates; the other, the anxious understanding that this attempt has failed. I consider the brain an organ of world making, where, through the material process of perception, the nervous system receives and responds to a world that it physically builds. I consider the brain cybernetic on account of the digital quality of the electrochemical action potential, a notion first put forward in Warren S. McCulloch and John Pfeiffer's "Of Digital Computers Called Brains" (1949). As David Bates has argued, there is a tradition in the history of science and technology of understanding the nervous system as both a cybernetic and open system, such that the recognition of the brain's technical structure does not preclude the recognition of adjustments required by neuroplasticity.[19] In the hallucinations associated with prion disease, whether outward efforts of flesh and charge ever meet a world is a question. In all likelihood, the impulses arch back like the venous sinusoids of the brain that drown their contents in the body's circulatory core.

In *Ontology of the Accident* (2012), Catherine Malabou describes a like kind of deepening interiority without recourse in relation to what she identifies as the destructive plasticity of brain injury: "an identity that . . . flees the impossibility of fleeing itself"; "an identity that does not subjectivize its [own] change."[20] In prion disease, there are psychic events, but there is also a materiality that attaches itself to the chronology of absconding subjectivity of which Malabou speaks. For example, patients with prion disease experience alien limb phenomenon, where limbs behave without the patient acknowledging that the limb now rising, now falling, is *their limb*.[21] Furthermore, in RT-QuIC assays,[22] you can watch prions "in real time create aggregates"[23] as a fluorescence of Thioflavin T, in a sample of nasal brushings from the infected patient. As a diagnostician, you watch as the light gets brighter.

To think through the material structure of the prion is not to reject the concept of information; rather, it is to envision a biomolecular world that is not mediated by language, where the information of reproduction is passed through the physical sculpting of one molecule by another such that information is "conformationally encoded" (FAM, 1). It is to offer a biological concept of information exchange without genetics and the protolinguistic processes of DNA transcription and mRNA translation that genetics requires. It is also to preserve medicine as a source of succor in the attempt to one day treat prion diseases, the spatial etiologies of which presently elude understanding.

N. Katherine Hayles, in *How We Became Posthuman: Virtual Bodies in Cybernetics, Literature, and Informatics*, describes how Maturana and Varela deprivileged the role of DNA with the concept of autopoiesis, where in the cell's attempt to reproduce its own organization, no one molecule is more important than another.[24] Evelyn Fox Keller, in *Refiguring Life: Metaphors of Twentieth-Century Biology*, argues that the association of gene and language is a product of discourse, what she terms the discourse of gene action; she traces the characterization of the gene from Schrödinger's discussion of gene as law code, through Watson and Crick's notion of information as genetic program, to Howard H. Pattee's critique of cybernetics, "How Does a Molecule Become a Message?"[25] With regard to work in twentieth-century philosophy of science that remained independent from a "discourse of gene-action" solely focused on the gene as an artifact of language, there is *The Strategy of the Genes*, by C. H. Waddington, which, in its concept of the epigenetic landscape, provides a model for how to analyze biological agents with attention to both the gene and its activity in space.[26]

Replicating apart from the gene, the prion propagates itself through form alone, requiring a philosophy of biology of space, whose object is spatial activity, whose focus is mimesis, or how form mimics form. Such a process in life can be recognized on scales greater than the microscopic: in Ovid's *Pygmalion*, where a sculptor attempts to make something real through form, and in the thought experiment in "Of Digital Computers Called Brains," where the authors suggest a piece-by-piece replacement of neurons by electrodes, to create "a relay having its own battery, charged by a series of chemical reactions converting sugar and oxygen to carbon dioxide and water,"[27] to set up an electrical device with the brain's own organization. If biology requires an effort to build our own forms, the prion shows how this occurs on a molecular level.

The Prion and Canguilhem's Biological Normativity

In Canguilhem's biology, form refers to both morphology and function, and a given morphology or a given function will be of negative value if it encumbers the polarity attributed to life.[28] For Canguilhem, "life is polarity" and norms exist as consequence, "express[ing] discriminations of qualities in conformity with the polar opposition of a positive and negative" (*NP*, 126, 240). Polarity concerns the orientational aspect of life, its directional quality, its preference, the fact that pathology as disease inheres in life as struggle.[29] The abnormal, whether it refers to the anatomically disfigured or the infirm, refers to a diminished ability to respond to a changing environment with norms, and like logical or ethical norms, the biological norm institutes an order by which other forms of order are devalued and rejected. The role of the biological norm is to "devalue existence by allowing its correction" (*NP*, 77). Examples from neuropathology are used in *The Normal and the Pathological*: patients with brain lesions who exhibit "a mania for order,"[30] "a downright taste for monotony,"[31] in reference to Kurt Goldstein's notion of the catastrophic reaction. The catastrophic reaction names the disorganized response of an organism to an environment that changes in such a way that the organism cannot accommodate the change. A narrowing of environment ensues, a desire for order and monotony, a meticulousness.[32] Canguilhem offers the example of the hemophiliac—in reference to the blood and not the brain—whose pathology reveals itself in the desire to keep separate the internal and external environments. Hypocoagulable and unclotted, the blood of the hemophiliac runs the same whether teeming from a paper cut or circulating in the aortic depths: "The hemorrhages are interminable."[33] Even though both the hemophiliac and the brain injured are abnormal in their function, they still abide by a norm they establish (the avoidance of objects that could penetrate the skin and a meticulously ordered environment, respectively), and so are *normal* in relation to what Canguilhem terms biological normativity: "Without being absurd, the pathological state can be called normal to the extent that it expresses a relationship to life's normativity" (*NP*, 227). Pathological norms are also vital norms, albeit of lessening value, for as is evident in the case of the brain injured and hemophiliac, instituting a norm of increased rigidity lessens the organism's ability to generate new norms in the case of a change in the environment. This lack of confidence in the organism's future normativity is determinative of what Canguilhem believes sickness to be: "The patient is sick because he can admit of only one norm. To use an expression which has already been very useful to us, the sick man is not abnormal because of the absence of a norm but because of his incapacity to be normative" (*NP*, 186). Even in pathological states, the living being will supply a new norm of diminished value in response to its environment—until the organism does not, until the organism dies.

Consider how the prion does not abide by Canguilhem's principle of biological normativity. There is no biology in which the prion does not replicate itself through its form; its vital norms will never not be transcendent among other norms. The prion does not die but builds and adds to itself ad infinitum. The prion *interminably* compresses and folds surrounding proteins, making its environment identical to itself, a hammer that is a mirror.

Outside the body, on the chrome of medical equipment, the prion is harder to kill than even the microbes of tuberculosis.[34] To kill the 8–91 micrograms of prion protein, identified as the PrPSc isoform, that would linger on a surgical instrument after a procedure, you must autoclave the instrument at 273.2°F for eighteen minutes.[35] With regard to the internal environment, the prion is not something the body is capable of stopping. The prion is resistant to the cellular proteases that in other circumstances unfurl and deactivate misfolded proteins and is resistant to physiological detergents.[36] What we would send after it does not impede it. If an infection occurs in the body, the prion, as a misfolded protein, will continuously misfold other proteins. The noninfectious proteins that the prion acts on acquire the prion's own form. Understanding biological normativity as the quality of the organism "for whom it is normal to break norms and establish new ones" (*NP*, 165), there is no norm of life the prion could establish that would not be sufficient in its environment; moreover, in transforming PrPC into PrPSc, the prion turns its environment into itself.

Vital norms in Canguilhem's system cannot be reduced to an average or to what traits are most common to a species; rather, if an average or common traits exist in a species, it is due to the differential evaluation of forms by life: "Life, using the variation of living forms, obtains a kind of insurance against specialization without reversibility" (*NP*, 142). It is form that is acted on by the process of biological normativity. Georges Teissier's butterflies serve as an example. Canguilhem analyzes the preponderance of black-colored butterflies that Teissier observed in cities. In industrialized regions, black-colored butterflies were observed to outnumber gray butterflies, but the results in forested regions were reversed. In forested regions the contrast of black coloring against vegetative green made the black butterfly more visible than the gray butterfly to the birds hunting them; however, in the cities of Europe, no longer threatened by their lack of camouflage, black butterflies flourished, benefiting from the speed the population developed while trying to flee avian predators. Canguilhem cites Henri Bergson on what such forest-earned agility achieves—"a powerlessness has been overcome" (NP, 143)—and describes the trait of speed in terms of preference, where the black butterfly exhibits the preferred form—a *normal form*, an *invention*.[37] Normalization occurs in an environment on the basis of an originary instability: an emergent form achieves a "synthetic harmony"[38] of anatomy and behavior that is temporary. The average, the form exhibited by the black butterfly and now the prion, is an expression of "the unstable equilibrium of nearly equal norms and forms of life temporarily brought together" (NP, 162). This near equality, this first fixity of form and value dropped out of a tincture, is always on the scale of myth because it is never *first*.

The norm, always presupposing other norms, has no origin story.[39] The norm depends on preexisting norms and also gains its regulatory force from its own infraction, which occurs after its introduction. There is a Janus-faced chronology to (1) a norm that will generate forms that devalue other forms and (2) the substitution and inversion of the norm that this makes possible. As evidence of a new norm and marker of biological value, a *new* form might come to displace the old. Canguilhem calls this displacement the *normal priority of infraction*, where "buil[t] into the relationship of the norm to its area of application" is the possibility of inversion (NP, 241); Canguilhem cites Kant on the experience of normative regulation, where the value of a rule cannot be enjoyed unless that rule is transcended by another rule's implementation. This ability of a norm to be transcended is what imbues a norm with its regulatory force. Canguilhem's counterexample is Golden Age Man, "paradisiacal man," who metes out life in a material environment that he neither builds nor is built by, where nature is "uncultivated, unprompted, unforced, unreclaimed" (NP, 241) and where there is no felt victory over the obstacle, no new norm, no infraction because there is no material insult to which the body must respond. Bearing a similarity to the noble savage, Canguilhem's golden age "paradisiacal man" (NP, 241) is ripe for critique, but at the same time Canguilhem acknowledges that *chaos* and the *golden age* are the stuff of myth: "Chaos and golden age are the mythical terms of the fundamental normative relation, terms so related that neither of the two can keep from turning into the other" (NP, 241). For chaos, Canguilhem refers to the earth of chaos in Ovid's *Metamorphoses*: "The earth of chaos does not bear fruit, the sea of chaos is not navigable, forms do not remain identical to themselves" (NP, 241). Chaos is offered as the formlessness that follows the absence of an identity relationship among biological objects, and the golden age, the "naive dream of regularity in the absence of rule" (NP, 241), as the absence of value attributed to the forms that biological objects take.

We can imagine the moments in evolutionary time that might correspond to the mythical terms of normativity that Canguilhem presents: the lightning strike that caused carbon chains to arrange themselves out from a primordial soup into self-propagating forms that we would term living[40] and a golden age of a future where medicine as a technique is no longer necessary. Even so, we live with the sense of something overhead, perhaps aware of a past when the sea covered the earth and an organizing principle in the form of DNA emerged from a reaction induced by lightning strike[41] or hyperthermic vent in the Marianas Trench.[42] Perhaps we are also aware that normative chaos is not necessarily behind us. The COVID-19 pandemic has made the uncertainty about our continued ability to impose our own organization, as "norms of life,"[43] on our environment ever more apparent. The image is of freezer trucks in the alleyways of New York hospitals, where only so much decay could be stopped by cold. Alternatively, the image is of the SARS-CoV-2 virus budding with new spike proteins, prompting the naming of a new variant, where taxonomy is as a holdfast. I argue that the prion's inability to be destroyed by the body and regular sterilization precautions, its ability to reproduce without DNA or RNA, and its ability to elude modern pharmacology—we have no cure—makes the uncertainty of whether biological chaos is before or behind us speakable. The point is not the fear; prion diseases are *rare*. The point is to determine what medicine is for, given the eventuality where our norms of life do not hold and our gene-based philosophy of biology can no longer explain what happens to life.

The Prion's Use of Space

PrPC is found in the brain on the surface of cells, but it has been found elsewhere: in the heart and spleen,[44] in the white blood cells of the immune system, the bone marrow.[45] Though the physiological function of the prion at these sites is "obscure" and our understanding "rudimentary," there are conjectures as to what the noninfectious isoform accomplishes in the body:[46] (1) maintaining the myelin sheath around neurons in the peripheral nervous system;[47] (2) facilitating the "self-renewal" of hematopoietic cells in the bone marrow (IPD, 889); (3) assisting in the phagocytosis of bacterium *Brucella abortus* (IPD, 889); (4) developing the differentiation of stem cells in an embryo (IPD, 889); and (5) enhancing the barrier function of microfold cells in the intestine (IPD, 889). Even so, "none of these functions has been unambiguously elucidated at a molecular level and conflicting results have often been reported" (IPD, 889). The prion gene is a conserved sequence, meaning that on an evolutionary scale, the genetic coding for the region of DNA referred to by the gene has remained unaltered in humans.[48] We have an illegible contract with it, with that which could disfigure us. Because we know so little and because we lack medical therapies for the prion-induced spongiform encephalopathies, prion research continues—but haltingly, due to the risks associated with the work. Prions are ineradicable by means of normal sterilization procedures, a durability attributed to the absence of DNA in the molecule.[49] We cannot inactivate prions by a scrambling of the code or by inhibiting the enzymes that would, in other microbes, work to reify that code. In fact, in July 2021 five French research institutions suspended prion-related research when one researcher at a site in Toulouse contracted

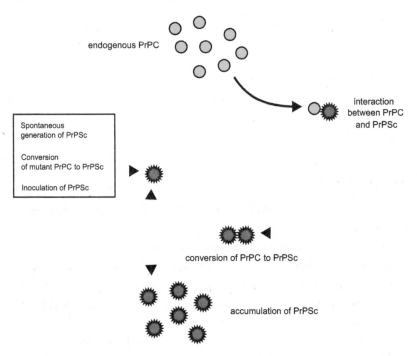

Fig. 3. Conversion to disordered form on contact.

Creutzfeldt-Jakob disease. This followed the postmortem diagnosis of another scientist, Émilie Jaumain, who died in 2019 after being cut by the forceps she was using to handle frozen sections of brain tissue from mice infected with bovine spongiform encephalitis.[50] Postmortem, prion disease could have been diagnosed the same way it is diagnosed in the living: by extracting a sample from the patient and then watching as the sample grows denser in disordered forms.[51] In the RT-QuIC procedure, the infectious prion protein (PrPSc) converts the PrPC to a form identical to itself (PrPSc-2), leading to an exponential growth in the amount of the disordered form. Each disordered form is identical to the form that rendered it, and these rendered forms go on to render others (fig. 3). This self-perpetuating feature has led some scientists to refer to the molecule as prionpropagon (IPD, 889).

But in normal times the prion floats in extracellular fluid, tied to the outside of a neuron by a protein that anchors it.[52] It was sent out, beating on the surface of the cell like a hair in water, with its protein attachment at the root. Before executing unknown functions at the surface, the prion is split three times:[53] the first is a bifurcation—now the prion has new ends; the second is an autocleave, where the polymer's own chemical constitution is responsible for removing molecules at one of the new poles within the most irregular conformation of the incipient structure—the helix breaker octapeptide repeats;[54] and the third and final split occurs at the amine end and sends N3 into the extracellular matrix, which I always imagined to have the density and tuftedness of a kelp forest.

Before surfacing, two ends of the prion are joined, and sulfur molecules form a bridge across the units—a disulfide bond.[55] The prion came from a ribosome, directed by an mRNA transcript, directed by a gene on chromosome 20.[56] The gene for the PrPC tendril at the surface of our neurons and the genetic code for PrPSc, whose aggregates destroy neurons without so much as an inflammatory response by the body, is the same: the one peacefully at rest in a microscopic ether, doing that which we do not know; the other, the infectious agent responsible for the spongiform encephalopathies—mad cow disease, Creutzfeldt-Jakob disease, kuru, scrapie—clotting itself with the clones it has produced, causing the neuron to rupture. The PRNP gene on chromosome 20 dictates the molecular constitution for both PrPC and PrPSc. The genetic code—the language at the center of the cell—is the same for the noninfectious and infectious isoform. And at the ribosome, the line of amino acids added end to end that serves as the basis of any protein, is the same. The dictation and the acolyte matter arranging itself on the basis of what came from the center are the same for both the noninfectious and the infectious isoform: the code and the atoms of each are the same. "PrPSc has the same primary structure as PrPC but a different fold."[57] The fold is the site of information exchange for the prion.

For every protein that is *not* a prion, the sites of information exchange are ribosomes and the cell nucleus, where mRNA is translated and DNA is transcribed. If a protein were not an infectious prion, it would be brought into being by a ribosome, which sits on a microcellular wall like a knot in an oak tree. The ribosome receives a single-stranded ribonucleic acid (RNA), which is code. As a specified arrangement of nitrogenous bases (adenosine, guanine, cytosine, uracil) in a linear order, the RNA is mRNA, messenger RNA, which has come out from the nucleus of the cell as a transcript, a traveling copy of code for one region of the DNA at the center of the cell. The transcription of DNA to mRNA takes place in the nucleus. The code is then translated into protein at the ribosome, where tRNAs like moths come and deposit amino acids in the prescribed order so that a protein obtains. Unlike this hypothetical protein, the prion is the agent of its own reproduction, as Jiyan and Wang suggest: "The 'protein-only hypothesis' provides a theoretical model to explain how a protein self-replicates without nucleic acid."[58] By "protein-only hypothesis" they refer to the theory that the prion, as an infectious agent, is constituted by itself alone, as opposed to the "virino hypothesis," a theory that the prion protein is joined with a nucleic acid that, as a codified representation of its structure, is the basis for its reproduction upon its entry to the cell; however, we know the prion has no nucleic acid, no code.[59] We know its structure reiterates among other objects in a manner not organized by genetic language, in a manner organized by molecular architecture alone. As mentioned, the prion information exchange occurs at a spatial site—a *fold*.

The Prion and Lefebvre's Critique of Language

For Henri Lefebvre in *Production of Space*, language is secondary to space, and when language is useful, its usefulness derives from the evolution of perception, when a tender body sensed a tumultuous world. He writes, "Perhaps the 'logicalness' intrinsic to articulated language operated from the start as a spatiality capable of bringing order to the qualitative chaos (the practico-sensory realm) presented by the perception of things,"[60] noting that language itself has a spatial quality attributable to bodily sensation. Privileging space over language, Lefebvre writes against what is referred to as the *priority of language thesis* while acknowledging the role that language, as a system, might have played in the inevitability of impressing oneself on one's environment: "those activities which mark the earth," "the traces," "organizing gestures and work performed in common" (*PS*, 17). But the critique of language is first posed as a question concerning logic, knowledge, and biology. Lefebvre writes, "Does language—logically, epistemologically, or genetically speaking—precede, accompany or follow social space?" (*PS*, 16). He writes of language with reference to the genetic code of DNA; he writes of language *genetically speaking*.

Lefebvre writes against the notion that the space of science and the space of mathematics, *mental space*, are spaces of the true, somehow unaffected by life. *Social space* refers to the space of the physical and the space of social practice and is counterposed to mental space. Lefebvre describes how mathematicians recognized that they could not account for how the theories of space they elaborated had consequences for social life ("The relationship between mathematics and reality—physical or social reality—was not obvious, and indeed a deep rift had developed between these two realms" [*PS*, 2]), how the problem of life in space was surrendered to philosophers to resolve. Lefebvre offers a critique of works in contemporary continental philosophy—those of Julia Kristeva, Jacques Derrida, and Roland Barthes—which he argues collapse mental space and the space of physical and social reality. At issue is the "presupposition of an identity between mental space (the space of philosophers and epistemologists) and real space" (*PS*, 6), the notion that an idea has come to organize life. As Lefebvre offers, there is no true space, but there are truths of space, which is a sentiment that is not paradoxical on account of Lefebvre's concept of production. There is a truth about the way in which space is produced. Space, "at once a precondition and a result of social superstructures" (*PS*, 85), while not a product like a kilogram of sugar or yard of cloth,[61] is still the effect of the transformation of raw material. Lefebvre offers, "The raw material of the production of space is not, as in the case of particular objects, a particular material: it is rather nature itself, nature transformed into a product, rudely manipulated, now threatened in its very existence, probably ruined and certainly—and most paradoxically— *localized*" (*PS*, 123). By *localized* I believe he means fixed as language fixes, localized as *made to speak*, in a positioning and arrangement, in the reconstructions of nature on the basis of social practice. As to how the localization of nature takes place, an example offered is the supplanting of tree rings by clocks, where nature as timekeeper is now made to speak through mechanism: "Lived time loses its form and its social interest—with the exception, that is, of time spent working" (PS, 95). This movement from the inscription of tree rings to the tick of clock hands should be understood as translation. In the same way that we can move nature's patterns into language, we can embed patterns as language in nature. With reference to pathways and networks, Lefebvre argues that the built environment under neocapitalism can be understood as a form of writing on nature, where instead of the mere translation of nature, we simply tell nature what it is through "imply[ing] a particular representation of space."[62] He was writing in 1991, and now the genetic revolution has so universalized its own mode of interpretation that to live is to read, and on a molecular scale: the scraps of matter that sustain life are understood not only as text but as text that can be worked on and edited.

The Nobel Prize–winning technology of CRISPR-Cas9 relies on the metaphor of gene editing to explain the activity of "precisely cutting DNA and then letting natural DNA repair processes . . . take over."[63] The metaphor of gene editing does not solely do explanatory work, however; it also affects the ways CRISPR-Cas9 and related gene-editing entities are experimented on, isolated, and monetized. One stock claiming a patent for CRISPR-Cas9 is abbreviated as EDIT, for *Editas*. More than how these biological entities are known, the metaphor of a correct language has dictated what these entities have become. They have been amplified, their linguistic function financially capitalized on and aggrandized.

For Lefebvre, language is what is used in the absence of knowledge of space[64] to misattribute qualities of social space to mental space, one of three fields that his theory of production attempts to unify (in addition to physical space and social space, there is the mental, which "include[es] logical and formal abstractions" [PS, 11]). At issue is the presumption that language is comprehensive in rendering clear what objects in space are. Language, whether through a nonrefusable invitation to self-disclosure of the object or through a voluminous outpouring of reality into code, according to Lefebvre "brings the non-communicated into the realm of the communicated—the *incommunicable* having no existence beyond that of an ever-pursued residue" (*PS*, 29). Lefebvre presents his critique of the ideology of speech, the "fetishism of the spoken word" and ideology of writing, "the fetishism of . . . writing" as a critique of the ideology of spatial transparency, and the notion that language, with its assumed "total clarity of communication," can be substituted for social practice, speaking more for life than life itself (*PS*, 28). Even so, in such ideologies, as in them all, what is incommunicable ferments as a residue identified by Lefebvre as extant yet ever pursued (*PS*, 28), a beguiling grime that renders comical the hierarchy established in the "grasping of the 'object' by the writing and speaking 'subject'" (*PS*, 28). Lefebvre writes in acknowledgment and support of a "pessimistic view of signs" (*PS*, 135), because in semiology or philosophy of language, social space is reduced to an inert stage[65] on which signs as pure utterances cavort and make meaning. Lefebvre articulates how space has activity that includes but is irreducible to the activity of language, how space has activity that, like the prion's spatial activity, cannot be approximated by semiotics or code.

Far from being inert, social space is "irreducible to a 'form' imposed on phenomena" (*PS*, 27), and its activity is explained in a metaphor from the discipline, fluid dynamics: "Great movements, vast rhythms, immense waves—these all collide and 'interfere' with one another; lesser movements, on the other hand, interpenetrate" (*PS*, 87). Even though social space operates by this principle of water, *the superimposition of small movements*, social space is not considered the space of environmental nature; rather, social space is considered the space of human practice, experienced by subjects as the space of life: "The behavior of their space is at once vital and mortal"; "within it they develop, give expression to themselves, and encounter prohibitions; then they perish, and that same space contains their graves" (*PS*, 34). Lefebvre seeks to recover how spatial practice has "disappear[ed] along with life" as contemporary philosophy has come to offer a "speculative primacy of the conceived over the lived" (*PS*, 34). Though the prion exists on a different scale than the cities on which Lefebvre writes, the idea that to take up space as a project allows us to somehow draw closer to life is an idea I agree with. As in biology, space reproduces itself.[66]

The Prion and Form

To visualize the process of prion reproduction, Giovanni Spagnolli et al. present an atomic model of the conversion of PrPC to PrPSc, observing how "the model we have created allowed us to perform the first reconstruction of how the information encoded into the conformation of a protein could be propagated in a directional fashion, a concept directly underlying the infectious nature of prions" (FAM, 8). Their infectious prion is a four-rung β-solenoid, a terraced and ladder-like molecule whose coils have been replaced with crêpey sheets. *Alpha-coils*, which are helices similar to DNA's double helix, and *Beta-sheets*, a zigzagging line of molecules that have been described to me as stackable like blocks of wood, are the two ways a chain of amino acids emerging from a ribosome can achieve structure of a higher order. Most proteins have an assortment of A-coils and B-sheets. PrPC has both; the infectious PrPSc protein does not.[67] Because each sheet is connected to the one below it, a solenoid develops on one curved end. Imagine two flags on their flagpoles but connected on the seam beating in the wind. The space between them is as a wind tunnel, and so the molecule *moves* (fig. 2). Whether you can discuss object permanence on the molecular level is a separate question answered in part by Heisenberg's uncertainty principle, but certainly with regard to proteins, anything you glimpse once will stretch or flex before you glimpse it again. The inherent biomolecular dynamism of all proteins is a process separate from the fundamental alteration of the tertiary structure of proteins, which is what takes place during prion conversion—when the infectious prion propagon takes the noninfectious isoform into its lowest rung and bends it. The rung is a conversion surface,[68] and "the prominent reaction mechanism is the sequential formation of rungs" (FAM, 7). This requires there to be an intermediate molecule before PrPC is transmuted completely (FAM, 7), so coil by coil the molecule is unspooled. Spagnolli et al. write about the chronology of propagon formation: "[This] first event initiates a cascade of conformational transitions in which each newly formed rung acts as a template for the formation of the following one, ultimately leading to the complete conversion of PrPC into PrPSc" (FAM, 7). After sculpting itself out of the material of another molecule, the prion aggregates itself with its replicated forms, threading the forms together as a fibril.[69]

At this stage, we now have a collection of ladder-like molecules woven into a fibril. The proteins of Parkinson's disease and Alzheimer's disease—the tau, α-synuclein, and amyloid beta plaques—demonstrate a similar kind of misfolding and aggregation. Described as a "prion-like seeded-polymerization,"[70] the proteins' self-replication is due to its prion-like architecture. Like prions, the gristle of the brain in Alzheimer's disease and Parkinson's disease, constituted by proteins arranging themselves into fibrils, can project its form on other forms. The model of prion propagation is presented explicitly as the folding of a protein within an energy landscape.[71] Because "a PrPSc aggregate can recruit PrPC proteins and can perpetuate its own amplification in a similar way to crystal growth and fragmentation" (IPD, 888), a prion can be understood as a crystal-in-life, a mimetic seed whose activity is potentially best approximated not by the regular terms of a biochemical reaction—enzyme, substrate, product—but instead by the terms of a *phase change*:[72] liquid, loss of entropy, crystalline structure.

Niccolò Candelise et al. describe prion protein aggregation as a phase change in which the threading of fibrils is modeled as an entropic conversion from liquid to solid. The beta sheets of the model oligomer, like those of the prion, "show no preference for chaperone binding"[73] and so elude the chaperones, the proteins that would otherwise facilitate the folding of the prion to a less energy-dense form. So, electrostatic, dense with charge, the sheets have no choice but to release energy as they are transformed and become threaded together. The model visualizes how intrinsically disordered proteins lose energy to become sheets. The charge is sunk into newly formed bonds; the beta sheets are demixed from the cytoplasm as a viscous gel. On the phase change: "The transition into a solid phase from a liquid droplet implies that a chaotic and disordered system (e.g., a liquid droplet) is organizing into ordered structures, reducing both the entropy of the system and the ability to exchange components with the environment."[74] Candelise et al. emphasize how proteins with intrinsically disordered regions like prions, after "transition[ing] into a more viscoelastic condensate," become unimpressible, immune to the demands of their environment; such misfolded proteins "eventually form gel-like structures no longer capable of exchanging components with the surrounding environment."[75] The prion is irremediable, a thing on which the environment has no pull, whereas Canguilhem, in *The Normal and the Pathological*, imagines the organism in *conversation* with its environment, in a metaphor that does not express a coded, signifying property of language as much as it expresses a tangled dynamism "where there are leaks, holes, escapes, and unexpected resistances."[76] Even here the understanding of language is as a material, an exchange that dilapidates by the efforts with which it is sustained. Certain organs in the cadaver lab evince this effort. I once saw an image of a heart on an anatomical tray after congestive heart failure. It was riven with holes, torn from its own attempts to maintain a beat. It looked like it had drowned.

Both the biologically abnormal and normal in *The Normal and the Pathological* respond to an environment. Even in pathology, understood as "organic disturbance," Canguilhem argues that we observe in ourselves and in others "new mode(s) of behavior for the organism relative to its environment" (*NP*, 87). There is an acknowledgment of the organism of its material surround, a nonindifference, a pain.[77] Seemingly, Canguilhem's materialism is best understood through a concept of environment because of the relationship of biological normativity to Darwin's concept of adaptation, with which Darwin articulates an evolved suitability of biological form to its surroundings. On the "habits of life"[78] that the giraffe demonstrates in its environment, Darwin writes: "The giraffe, by its lofty stature, much elongated neck, fore legs, head and tongue, has its whole frame beautifully adapted for browsing on the higher branches of trees."[79] Canguilhem acknowledges a certain permissiveness of the environment to make livable a "variety of forms"[80] that offer any given organism *fertility*—which should be understood not as reproductive capacity but as the possibility to change form; however, Canguilhem disagrees with the requirement of the theory of adaptation that the environment is a *given*, "an already constituted fact" (*NP*, 283).

In a critique of the theory of adaptation, Canguilhem presents the following:

In [all interpretations of the concept of adaptation] the environment is considered as a physical fact, not as a biological fact, as
an already constituted fact and not as a fact to be constituted.
By contrast, if the organism-environment relation is considered
as the effect of a really biological activity, as the search for a situation in which the living being receives, instead of submits to,
influences and qualities which meet its demands, then the environments in which living beings find themselves are carved out by
them, centered on them. In this sense the organism is not thrown
into an environment to which he must submit, but he structures
his environment at the same time that he develops his capacities
as an organism. (NP, 283)

For Canguilhem, the environment is the "work of the living being,"[81]
and though biological normativity indirectly acts on the organism's
environment, I argue that it directly acts on form. I argue that form is
the central concept of Canguilhem's materialism. Form is what is
elaborated by life as a technical, normative process. For Canguilhem,
life is originary technique,[82] a way: "All human technique, including
that of life, is set within life, that is, within an activity of information
and assimilation of material" (NP, 130). Life is a technique of elabo-
rating forms that all other techniques—including the technique of
medicine—are set within.

   Furthermore, the history of form—the history of anatomy—is the
science that precedes Canguilhem's biological normativity. Particularly, in the chapter titled "A Critical Examination of Certain Concepts," Canguilhem demonstrates interest in teratology, the history
of anatomical anomalies. Considering what an anatomical anomaly
is, Canguilhem determines that it is an empirical concept.[83] The
anomaly is there. The heart is on the right side.[84] There is a cervical
rib.[85] The spleen is missing.[86] The bowel is looped and malrotated.[87]
The term anomaly is a "description of biological fact,"[88] in contrast
to the term abnormal, "which implies reference to a value" (NP, 132).
And the anomaly might not even be a deformity—that is, it might not
even be visible: "The anomaly is ignored insofar as there is no manifestation of it in the order of vital values" (NP, 135). Canguilhem is
careful to mark how we name the process of biological normativity
from how we name the shape of the body, likely because one, the

process, comes to affect the other, the shape. The organism that exhibits biological normativity "displac[es] all withered, obsolete, and perhaps soon to be extinct forms" (*NP*, 144). Though we can consider the process on an evolutionary timescale, we can also consider the process of biological normativity originating in the blood vessels of an individual body. What if a norm were a reused injection site, where something comes to induce matter to generate forms? If we were to imagine the norm as an injection site, a site for entry of IV fluids and pharmacology, which then take shape in the body, causing certain changes—infection recovery, anesthetic sleep before surgery—we could then see how *norm* itself could be a spatial term.

Conclusion: "Disease Enters and Leaves Man as Through a Door" (*NP*, 39)

In *Subtraction*, by the architect and theorist Keller Easterling, we are presented with what I interpret as a model of biological normativity in the built environment. Easterling's argument is that the subtraction of buildings, which in Canguilhem's biology would be the rejection of forms by the normal organism, is as productive as the process of secreting buildings into existence because both the building and the removal of the built environment release "active forms," understood as "multipliers, switches, remote controls or governors—time released protocols that generate or manage . . . exchanges with a stream of objects and spaces."[89] She describes the demolition of buildings, the volatility of financial markets that "surround seemingly static and durable structures," the tabula rasa that is the "weapon of the patient urban magistrate or planner who claims to be cleansing and purifying diseased fabric," the Chernobyl disaster, and the "unbuilding projects" of urban Detroit as examples of spatial subtraction understood as a violence that is not solely negative (*S*, 1, 5, 17). Subtraction, like the death of the organism on an evolutionary timescale, is not solely a process of disappearance and loss[90]—it is a process of disappearance and loss that instantiates or solidifies an order for life.

Against Easterling's active forms, which "interact, evolve and unfold in dialogue with the world around them" (*S*, 39), and against Canguilhem's organism whose responsiveness to the world is its means of sustaining life, dripping value from a norm,[91] there is the prion (PrPSc), from which nothing can be elicited but its own form, interminably projected on other proteins found in the tissue of the nervous system. Because of the characteristics of the energy landscape the prion self-replicates within, because the prion can be modeled as a solid crystal dropping out of a liquid solution,[92] PrPC conversion to PrPSc is the thermodynamically favored reaction. It is unstoppable. Once a single PrPSc seed is introduced, it will sculpt other proteins in its own image, in a process of iterative misfolding unabated by the body. To accomplish this process of self-propagation, the prion PrPSc does not seek recourse to DNA, the genetic language at the center of the cell, responsible for all other cellular processes of biological self-propagation. I have argued that the prion abides neither by the principle of biological normativity nor by a philosophy of biology that understands life on the basis of code, and so requires an examination of Canguilhem's materialism, how space and form are understood in *The Normal and the Pathological*, and a sketch of a philosophy of biology that privileges space over language, whose central term is not gene but form. Proteins become prions through a fold.

The Normal and the Pathological was published in 1943, but it was republished in 1966, after the genetic revolution. In the republication Canguilhem considers genetically determined blood diseases in relation to language, where contorted blood cells are caused by a textual misinterpretation: "If, in principle, organization is a kind of language, the genetically determined disease is no longer a mischievous curse but a misunderstanding" (*NP*, 278). The shape is ordered by language but by a language from nowhere: "Here we are dealing with a word which comes from no mouth, with a writing which comes from no hand" (*NP*, 278). This nothingness with a voice leads us to what I believe is Canguilhem's cause for studying medicine—*for we get sick "in order to not lose all hope"*[93]—to resolve the horror that we live on the basis of information we neither control nor understand.

....

KATHLEEN POWERS is a medical student at the University of California, Irvine, School of Medicine. She graduated from the doctoral program in rhetoric at the University of California, Berkeley, and studies the organism in philosophy of biology.

Acknowledgments

I thank Keller Easterling and James C. Scott, for in their respective Yale College courses "Globalization Space" and "Rivers," I became aware of a new way of seeing.

Notes

1. Diffusion weighted refers to a type of magnetic resonance imaging (MRI) that evaluates the activity of water molecules in the brain.
2. Stern-Nezer, "Creutzfeldt-Jakob Disease Clinical Case."
3. Stern-Nezer, "Creutzfeldt-Jakob Disease Clinical Case."
4. Stern-Nezer, "Creutzfeldt-Jakob Disease Clinical Case."
5. Referring to the crêpey Beta-sheets of the four-rung β-solenoid. Spagnolli et al., "Full Atomistic Model of Prion Structure and Conversion," 1 (hereafter cited as FAM). There are viruses that reproduce on the basis of RNA without the presence of DNA. Both RNA and DNA are nucleic acids and function on the basis of a shared nitrogenous base code, with the exception of uracil's use in RNA and thymine's use in DNA. As Spagnolli et al. emphasize, the prion contains neither DNA nor RNA and so exists in a category apart from other known infectious agents ("Full Atomistic Model of Prion Structure and Conversion"). The prion reproduces without the function of RNA's and DNA's base-pairing code. Throughout this essay I refer to DNA, but, where applicable, I use it to refer to both nucleic acids of the genetic code.
6. See, e.g., Villarreal, "Are Viruses Alive?"; Van Regenmortel and Mahy, "Emerging Issues in Virus Taxonomy"; and Postgate, *Microbes and Man*.
7. See Geroulanos and Meyers, *Human Body*.
8. See Scott, *Seeing Like a State*; and Gissen, *Subnature*.
9. "A knockout mouse is a laboratory mouse in which researchers have inactivated, or 'knocked out,' an existing gene by replacing it or disrupting it with an artificial piece of DNA" (National Human Genome Research Institute, "Knockout Mice Fact Sheet").
10. Aguzzi, Nuvolone, and Zhu, "The Immunobiology of Prion Diseases" (hereafter cited as IPD).
11. Referring to variably protease-sensitive prionopathy, Appleby and Cohen write, "As with all prion diseases, the disease is universally fatal and there are no effective treatments" ("Diseases of the Central Nervous System Caused by Prions").

12. The Heidenhain variant in particular is known to cause hallucinations. See Sokhi et al., "Heidenhain Variant of Sporadic Creutzfeldt-Jakob Disease," 39.

13. Sokhi et al., "Heidenhain Variant of Sporadic Creutzfeldt-Jakob Disease," 39.

14. Brar, Vaddigiri, and Scicutella, "Of Illusions, Hallucinations, and Creutzfeldt-Jakob Disease," 124.

15. Badrfam et al., "Creutzfeldt-Jakob Disease after Dental Procedure," 107.

16. Brar, Vaddigiri, and Scicutella, "Of Illusions, Hallucinations, and Creutzfeldt-Jakob Disease," 124.

17. Klotz and Penfold, "Low Mood, Visual Hallucinations, and Falls."

18. Badrfam et al., "Creutzfeldt-Jakob Disease after Dental Procedure," 107.

19. Bates, "Automaticity."

20. Malabou, Ontology of the Accident, 11.

21. Ciarlariello et al., "Arm Levitation"; Rubin et al., "Alien Limb Phenomenon."

22. Orrú et al., "Test for Creutzfeldt-Jakob Disease."

23. Stern-Nezer, "Creutzfeldt-Jakob Disease Clinical Case."

24. Hayles, How We Became Posthuman; Maturana and Varela, Autopoiesis and Cognition.

25. Fox Keller, Refiguring Life; Schrödinger, What Is Life?; Watson and Crick, "Genetical Implications of the Structure of Deoxyribonucleic Acid"; Pattee, "How Does a Molecule Become a Message?"

26. Waddington, Strategy of the Genes.

27. McCulloch and Pfeiffer, "Of Digital Computers Called Brains," 369.

28. "As long as the morphological or functional variations on the specific type do not hinder or subvert this polarity, the anomaly is a tolerated fact; in the opposite case the anomaly is felt as having negative vital value and is expressed as such on the outside" (Canguilhem, The Normal and the Pathological, 136 [hereafter cited as NP]).

29. "Even for an amoeba, living means preference and exclusion. A digestive tract, sexual organs, constitute an organism's behavioral norms. Psychoanalytic language is indeed right to give the name poles to the natural orifices of ingestion and excretion. A function does not work indifferently in several directions. A need places the proposed objects of satisfaction in relation to propulsion and repulsion. There is a dynamic polarity of life" (NP, 136). "We think that medicine exists as the art of life because the

living human being himself calls certain dreaded states or behaviors pathological (hence requiring avoidance or correction) relative to the dynamic polarity of life, in the form of a negative value. We think that in doing this the living human being extends a spontaneous effort, peculiar to life, to struggle against that which obstructs its preservation and development taken as norms" (*NP*, 126).

30. "Hence the mania for order and meticulousness of these patients, their downright taste for monotony and their attachment to a situation they know they can dominate" (*NP*, 186). "What Goldstein pointed out in his patients is the establishment of new norms of life by a reduction in their level of activity as related to a new but *narrowed* environment. The narrowing of the environment in patients with cerebral lesions corresponds to their impotence in responding to the demands of the normal, that is, previous environment" (*NP*, 185).

31. See n. 30.

32. See n. 30.

33. "But the hemorrhages are interminable, as if the blood were indifferent to its situation inside or outside the vessels" (*NP*, 140).

34. Goldin, "Sterilization and Disinfection."

35. Sakudo, "Inactivation Methods for Prions."

36. Gill and Castle, "The Cellular and Pathologic Prion Protein."

37. "We may well ask whether there wouldn't be a kind of general rule for the invention of living forms" (*NP*, 162).

38. "A normal specific form would be the product of a normalization between functions and organs whose synthetic harmony is obtained in defined conditions and is not given" (*NP*, 162).

39. Canguilhem describes how the norm of *perfect health* does not exist even if its material result exists as a form preferred among others: "A norm does not exist, it plays its role which is to devalue existence by allowing its correction" (*NP*, 77). And this nonexistence of perfect health is not because perfect health is necessarily unattainable but because the norm fails to be the source of its own existence. The norm itself does not comprise an origin story. It is described in an analogy of the perfect being: the perfect being does not exist because—on account of the quality *perfection*—it is incapable of explaining or materially accounting for its own coming into being. The same with the *concept of perfect health*: "For a long time people tried to find out whether they could prove the existence of the perfect being starting with its quality of perfection, since, having all the perfections, it would also have that of

bringing about its own existence. The problem of the actual existence of perfect health is analogous" (*NP*, 77).

40. J. B. S. Haldane's 1929 essay "Origin of Life" documents the experiments of the primordial soup theory. See Tirard, "J. B. S. Haldane and the Origin of Life."

41. See n. 40.

42. Plümper et al., "Subduction Zone Forearc Serpentinites."

43. "There is no fact which is normal or pathological in itself. An anomaly or mutation is not in itself pathological. These two express other possible norms of life" (*NP*, 144).

44. Gill and Castle, "The Cellular and Pathologic Prion Protein."

45. See the discussion of mice bone marrow transplantation experiments in IPD.

46. "The prion protein is a relatively small glycoprotein that is tethered to the outer leaflet of the plasma membrane, where it appears to interact with various molecular partners to carry out what is currently rather an obscure function" (Gill and Castle, "The Cellular and Pathologic Prion Protein," 21). "The elucidation of the physiological functions of PrPC is rudimentary" (IPD, 889).

47. "In peripheral nerves, PrPC contributes to myelin maintenance" (IPD, 889).

48. Gill and Castle, "The Cellular and Pathologic Prion Protein," 21.

49. Sakudo, "Inactivation Methods for Prions."

50. Casassus, "France Issues Moratorium on Prion Research."

51. Satoh et al., "Postmortem Quantitative Analysis."

52. Gill and Castle, "The Cellular and Pathologic Prion Protein."

53. "During its life cycle, a PrPC molecule can undergo up to three cleavage events, the functional and pathologic significance of which are still under investigation" (Gill and Castle, "The Cellular and Pathologic Prion Protein," 22).

54. "This region incorporates several imperfect, glycine/proline-rich octapeptide repeats that contribute to the flexibility of the N-terminal region" (Gill and Castle, "The Cellular and Pathologic Prion Protein," 25).

55. A disulfide bond in the C-terminal domain. See Gill and Castle, "The Cellular and Pathologic Prion Protein."

56. Gill and Castle, "The Cellular and Pathologic Prion Protein."

57. Chen, van der Kamp, and Daggett, "Structural and Dynamic Properties of the Human Prion Protein," 1152.

58. Ma and Wang, "Prion Disease and the 'Protein-Only Hypothesis.'"

59. "Since poly(rA) does not contain meaningful genetic information, the . . . experiment reveals that the role of poly(rA) is to facilitate PrP conformational change instead of providing genetic information for the infectivity, and disproves the 'virino hypothesis'" (Ma and Wang, "Prion Disease and the 'Protein-Only Hypothesis,'" 188).

60. Lefebvre, *The Production of Space*, 17 (hereafter cited as *PS*).

61. "Space is never produced in the sense that a kilogram of sugar or a yard of cloth is produced" (*PS*, 85).

62. "Traversed now by pathways and patterned by networks, natural space changes: one might say that practical activity writes upon nature, albeit in a scrawling hand, and that this writing implies a particular representation of space" (*PS*, 117).

63. CRSPR Therapeutics, "CRSPR/Cas9."

64. "There are plenty of reasons for thinking that descriptions and cross-sections of this kind, though they may well supply inventories of what *exists in* space, or even generate a *discourse on* space, cannot ever give rise to *a knowledge of space*. And, without such a knowledge, we are bound to transfer onto the level of discourse, of language per se—i.e. the level of mental space—a large portion of the attributes and 'properties' of what is actually social space" (*PS*, 7).

65. "It [space] has of course always been the reservoir of resources, and the medium in which strategies are applied, but it has now become something more than the theatre, the disinterested stage or setting, of action. Space does not eliminate the other materials or resources that play a part in the socio-political arena, be they raw materials or the most finished of products, be they businesses or 'culture.' Rather, it brings them all together and then in a sense substitutes itself for each factor separately by enveloping it" (*PS*, 410).

66. For Lefebvre, the reproduction of space is a Marxist concept related to the reproduction of the means of production: "The diversion and re-appropriation of space are of great significance, for they teach us much about the production of new spaces. During a period as difficult as the present one is for a (capitalist) mode of production which is threatened with extinction yet struggling to win a new lease on life (through the reproduction of the means of production), it may even be that such techniques of diversion have greater import than attempts at creation (production)" (*PS*, 167).

67. See the discussion of FTIR spectroscopy in FAM, 2.

68. "The associated rMD simulations yielded a transition pathway with full atomistic resolution in which the C-terminal rung of the solenoid acts as a primary conversion surface for PrPC unstructured N-terminus (residues 89–124)" (FAM, 7).

69. "All these constraints were comprehensively included into a 2D threading scheme spanning mouse PrP (moPrP) residues 89–230 (S1 Fig), also considering the structural propensities of different residues: polyglycine tracts and prolines were positioned in loops due to their destabilizing effects on β-strands" (FAM, 3).

70. Baiardi et al., "Recent Advances," 278.

71. Candelise et al., "Protein Aggregation Landscape."

72. Candelise et al. use the term *phase transition*: "The cellular milieu is an environment crowded with macromolecules . . . within this crowded medium with very little available space. . . . Dynamic interactions between IDRs [intrinsically disordered regions] and other molecules, according to the polyvalent electrostatic model, allow for condensation and phase transition" ("Protein Aggregation Landscape").

73. Candelise et al., "Protein Aggregation Landscape."

74. Candelise et al., "Protein Aggregation Landscape."

75. Candelise et al., "Protein Aggregation Landscape."

76. "For the living being life is not a monotonous deduction, a rectilinear movement, it ignores geometrical rigidity, it is discussion or explanation (what Goldstein calls *Auseinandersetzung*) with an environment where there are leaks, holes, escapes, and unexpected resistances" (*NP*, 198).

77. On nonindifference: "We . . . think that the fact that a living man reacts to a lesion, infection, functional anarchy by means of a disease expresses the fundamental fact that life is not indifferent to the conditions in which it is possible; that life is polarity and thereby even an unconscious position of value; in short, life is in fact a normative activity" (*NP*, 126). On pain: "It seems that one must above all carefully distinguish pain of integumentary (surface) origin from pain of visceral origin. If the latter is presented as abnormal, it seems difficult to dispute the normal character of pain which arises at the surface of the organism's separation from as well as encounter with the environment. The suppression of integumentary pain in scleroderma or syringomyelia can lead to the organism's indifference to attacks on its integrity" (*NP*, 98).

78. "Thus, community in embryonic structure reveals community of descent; but dissimilarity in development does not prove discommunity

of descent, for in one of two groups, the developmental stages may have been suppressed or may have been so greatly modified through adaptations to new habits of life, as to no longer be recognizeable" (*NP*, 200). For a comparison of habit and instinct and a discussion of whether each is inherited, see also Darwin, *Origin of Species*, chap. 7.

79. Darwin, *Origin of Species*, 177.

80. "For any given form of life the environment is normal to the extent that it allows it fertility and a corresponding variety of forms such that, should changes in the environment occur, life will be able to find the solution to the problem of adaptation—which it has been brutally forced to resolve—in one of these forms" (*NP*, 143).

81. "In fact the environment of the living being is also the work of the living being who chooses to shield himself from or submit himself to certain influences" (*NP*, 179).

82. See n. 83.

83. "It is clear that, so defined, anomaly is, generally speaking, a purely empirical or descriptive concept, a statistical deviation" (*NP*, 133).

84. "The heart on the right-hand side is no myth" (*NP*, 134).

85. Comparing anomaly to monstrosity: "It goes without saying that a cervical rib is a simpler anomaly than ectromelia" (*NP*, 134).

86. See n. 87, also in reference to heterotaxies.

87. "*Heterotaxies*, a term created by Geoffroy Saint-Hilaire, are complex anomalies, serious in appearance in terms of the anatomical relationship, but they impede no function and are not apparent on the outside" (*NP*, 133).

88. "Geoffroy Saint-Hilaire, who makes the etymological error, repeated after him by Littré and Robin, tries to maintain the purely descriptive and theoretical meaning of 'anomaly,' which is a biological fact and must be treated as such" (*NP*, 132).

89. Easterling, *Subtraction*, 3 (hereafter cited as *S*).

90. "Subtraction generally signals loss while accumulation or accretion generally signals growth. And when building is the only proper, sanctioned event, there is no platform in place for constructively handling the deletions that reasonably or unreasonably accompany building . . . but a subtraction economy that removes building must also deploy active forms" (*S*, 2).

91. "If biological norms exist it is because life, as not only subject to the environment but also as an institution of its own environment, thereby posits values not only in the environment but also in the organism itself. This is what we call biological normativity" (*NP*, 227).

92. See the discussion of Candelise et al.'s energetic model of the prion ("Protein Aggregation Landscape") as well as n. 72 for Aguzzi, Nuvolone, and Zhu's characterization in their review of the literature.

93. "We can hope to conquer disease even if it is the result of a spell, or magic, or possession; we have only to remember that disease happens to man in order not to lose all hope," Canguilhem, (*NP*, 39).

References

Aguzzi, Adriano, Mario Nuvolone, and Caihong Zhu. "The Immunobiology of Prion Diseases." *Nature Reviews Immunology* 13, no. 12 (2013): 888–902.

Appleby, Brian S., and Mark L. Cohen. "Diseases of the Central Nervous System Caused by Prions." *UpToDate*, May 19, 2021. www.uptodate.com/contents/diseases-of-the-central-nervous-system-caused-by-prions.

Badrfam, Rahim, Ahmad Ali Noorbala, Zahra Vahabi, and Atefeh Zandifar. "Creutzfeldt-Jakob Disease after Dental Procedure along with the Initial Manifestations of Psychiatric Disorder: A Case Report." *Iranian Journal of Psychiatry* 16, no. 1 (2021): 106–10.

Baiardi, Simone, Marcello Rossi, Sabina Capellari, and Piero Parchi. "Recent Advances in the Histo-molecular Pathology of Human Prion Disease." *Brain Pathology* 29, no. 2 (2019): 278–300.

Bates, David. "Automaticity, Plasticity, and the Deviant Origins of Artificial Intelligence." In *Plasticity and Pathology: On the Formation of the Neural Subject*, edited by David Bates and Nima Bassiri, 194–218. New York: Fordham University Press, 2015.

Brar, Harpal K., Vaishnavi Vaddigiri, and Angela Scicutella. "Of Illusions, Hallucinations, and Creutzfeldt-Jakob Disease (Heidenhain's Variant)." *Journal of Neuropsychiatry and Clinical Neurosciences* 17, no. 1 (2005): 124–26.

Candelise, Niccolò, Silvia Scaricamazza, Illari Salvatori, Alberto Ferri, Cristiana Valle, Valeria Manganelli, Tina Garofalo, Maurizio Sorice, and Roberta Misasi. "Protein Aggregation Landscape in Neurodegenerative Diseases: Clinical Relevance and Future Applications." *International Journal of Molecular Sciences* 22, no. 11 (2021). doi.org/10.3390/ijms22116016.

Canguilhem, Georges. *The Normal and the Pathological*, translated by Carolyn Fawcett. New York: Zone, 1989.

Casassus, Barbara. "France Issues Moratorium on Prion Research after Fatal Brain Disease Strikes Two Lab Workers." *Science*, July 28, 2021. www

.science.org/news/2021/07/france-issues-moratorium-prion-research
-after-fatal-brain-disease-strikes-two-lab.

Chen, Wei, Marc W. van der Kamp, and Valerie Daggett. "Structural and Dynamic Properties of the Human Prion Protein." *Biophysical Journal* 106, no. 5 (2014): 1152–63.

Ciarlariello, Vinícius Boaratti, Orlando G. P. Barsottini, Alberto J. Espay, and José Luiz Pedroso. "Arm Levitation as Initial Manifestation of Creutzfeldt-Jakob Disease: Case Report and Review of the Literature." *Tremor and Other Hyperkinetic Movements* 8 (2018). www.ncbi.nlm.nih.gov/pmc/articles/PMC6377915.

CRSPR Therapeutics. "CRSPR/Cas9." September 25, 2021. www.crisprtx.com/gene-editing/crispr-cas9.

Darwin, Charles. *The Origin of Species by Means of Natural Selection.* Cambridge: Cambridge University Press, 2009.

Easterling, Keller. *Subtraction.* Cambridge, MA: MIT Press for Sternberg Press, 2014.

Fox Keller, Evelyn. *Refiguring Life: Metaphors of Twentieth-Century Biology.* New York: Columbia University Press, 1995.

Geroulanos, Stefanos, and Todd Meyers. *The Human Body in the Age of Catastrophe: Brittleness, Integration, Science, and the Great War.* Chicago: University of Chicago Press, 2018.

Gill, Andrew C., and Andrew R. Castle. "The Cellular and Pathologic Prion Protein." *Handbook of Clinical Neurology* 153 (2018): 21–44.

Gissen, David. *Subnature: Architecture's Other Environments.* Princeton, NJ: Princeton University Press, 2009.

Goldin, Alan. "Sterilization and Disinfection." Lecture presented for the course "Medical Microbiology," University of California, Irvine, School of Medicine, August 26, 2021.

Hayles, N. Katherine. *How We Became Posthuman: Virtual Bodies in Cybernetics, Literature, and Informatics.* Chicago: University of Chicago Press, 1999.

Klotz, Daniel Martin, and Rose Sarah Penfold. "Low Mood, Visual Hallucinations, and Falls—Heralding the Onset of Rapidly Progressive Probable Sporadic Creutzfeldt-Jakob Disease in a Seventy-Three-Year-Old: A Case Report." *Journal of Medical Case Reports* 12, no. 1 (2018). doi.org/10.1186/s13256-018-1649-4.

Lefebvre, Henri. *The Production of Space*, translated by Donald Nicholson-Smith. London: Blackwell, 1991.

Ma, Jiyan, and Fei Wang. "Prion Disease and the 'Protein-Only Hypothesis.'" *Essays in Biochemistry* 56 (2014): 181–91.

Malabou, Catherine. *Ontology of the Accident: An Essay on Destructive Plasticity*, translated by Carolyn Shread. Cambridge: Polity, 2012.

Maturana, Humberto R., and Francisco J. Varela. *Autopoiesis and Cognition: The Realization of the Living*. Dordrecht: Reidel, 1980.

McCulloch, Warren, and John Pfeiffer. "Of Digital Computers Called Brains." *Scientific Monthly* 69, no. 6 (1949): 368–76.

Mead, Simon, and Peter Rudge. "CJD Mimics and Chameleons." *Practical Neurology* 17, no. 2 (2017): 113–21.

National Human Genome Research Institute. "Knockout Mice Fact Sheet." August 17, 2020. www.genome.gov/about-genomics/fact-sheets/knock out-mice-fact-sheet.

Orrú, Christina D., et al. "A Test for Creutzfeldt-Jakob Disease Using Nasal Brushings." *New England Journal of Medicine* 371, no. 6 (2014): 519–29.

Pattee, Howard H. "How Does a Molecule Become a Message?" *Developmental Biology Supplement* 3 (1969): 1–16.

Plümper, Oliver, Helen E. King, Thorsten Geisler, Yang Liu, Sonja Pabst, Ivan P. Savov, Detlef Rost, and Thomas Zack. "Subduction Zone Forearc Serpentinites as Incubators for Deep Microbial Life." *Proceedings of the National Academy of Sciences* 114, no. 17 (2017): 4324–29.

Postgate, John. *Microbes and Man*. Cambridge: Cambridge University Press, 2000.

Rubin, Mark, Jonathan Graff-Radford, Bradley Boeve, Keith A. Josephs, and Allen J Aksamit. "The Alien Limb Phenomenon and Creutzfeldt-Jakob Disease." *Parkinsonism and Related Disorders* 18, no. 7 (2012): 842–46.

Sakudo, Akikazu. "Inactivation Methods for Prions." *Current Issues in Molecular Biology* 36 (2020): 23–32.

Satoh, Katsuya, et al. "Postmortem Quantitative Analysis of Prion Seeding Activity in the Digestive System." *Molecules* 24, no. 24 (2019). doi.org/10.3390/molecules24244601.

Schrödinger, Erwin. *What Is Life?* Cambridge: Cambridge University Press, 1944.

Scott, James C. *Seeing Like a State: How Certain Schemes to Improve the Human Condition Have Failed*. New Haven, CT: Yale University Press, 1999.

Sokhi, Dilraj, Fazal Yakub, Karishma Sharma, Sheila Waa, and Peter Mativo. "Heidenhain Variant of Sporadic Creutzfeldt-Jakob Disease: First Reported Case from East Africa." *International Medical Case Reports Journal* 14 (2021): 39–44.

142   QUI PARLE   JUNE 2022   VOL. 31 NO. 1

Spagnolli, Giovanni, Simone Orioli, Alejandro M. Sevillano, Pietro Faccioli, Holger Wille, Emiliano Biasini, and Jesús R. Requena. "Full Atomistic Model of Prion Structure and Conversion." *PLoS Pathogens* 15, no. 7 (2019). doi.org/10.1371/journal.ppat.1007864.

Stern-Nezer, Sara. "Creutzfeldt-Jakob Disease Clinical Case." Lecture presented for the course "Medical Biochemistry and Molecular Cell Biology," University of California, Irvine, School of Medicine, March 29, 2021.

Tirard, Stéphane. "J. B. S. Haldane and the Origin of Life." *Journal of Genetics* 96, no. 5 (2017): 735–39.

Van Regenmortel, Marc H. V., and Brian W. J. Mahy. "Emerging Issues in Virus Taxonomy." *Emerging Infectious Diseases* 10, no. 1 (2004): 8–13.

Villarreal, Luis P. "Are Viruses Alive?" *Scientific American*, August 8, 2008. www.scientificamerican.com/article/are-viruses-alive-2004.

Waddington, C. H. *The Strategy of the Genes*. London: Allen and Unwin, 1957.

Watson, J. D., and F. Crick. "Genetical Implications of the Structure of Deoxyribonucleic Acid." *Nature* 171 (1953): 964–67.

Starships and Slave Ships

Black Ontology and the UFO Abduction Phenomenon

JONATHAN JACOB MOORE

For sure—uncanny to consider those ships kin
or kith—but we *are* out the same factory
   Douglas Kearney

Evidence suggests that the UFO/alien abduction phenomenon is
exclusively experienced by white people in the United States. But
while scholars have probed abductee narratives to surface political
and symbolic anxieties for decades, none have thought of the phenomenon's whiteness alongside the archival absence of Black abductees.

Using abductee accounts, interdisciplinary studies of the UFO
abduction phenomenon, and critiques of Black subjectivity, this article attends to the ontological anxieties that permeate UFO abduction
narratives and their choreographic resonance with the psychoso-
matics of Black life.

This article begins by examining the exceptional narrative of
Barney Hill, America's first and thus far only popular Black abductee. Then it brings into focus UFOlogy's aporetic negation of racial
subjectivity and suggests that the UFO abduction phenomenon is,

QUI PARLE   Vol. 31, No. 1, June 2022
DOI 10.1215/10418385-9669525   © 2022 Editorial Board, *Qui Parle*

a posteriori, inaccessible to the Black nonsubject. Finally, it returns to Hill's experience and offers speculative implications of a libidinal relationship between the starship's technics and the slave ship's terror.

Captivation

Abduction was imminent. It was September 19, 1961, sixty degrees, and the sky was clear. A day before the Hills' journey, three Black first-year students had integrated Georgia Tech. Four months earlier a mob had gleefully brutalized Congress of Racial Equity activists as they arrived by bus in Montgomery. And before being taken aboard the UFO that had stalked him and his white wife, Betty, from the sky as they drove from Montreal to their home in Portsmouth, New Hampshire, Barney Hill feared that he could not defend them by sheer will alone. His straight-ahead stare prevented the occupants of passing cars from noticing the sweat on his brow. He took solace in the gun hidden in his trunk.

The surprise "honeymoon" trip to Niagara Falls, nearly sixteen months after the couple's marriage, delighted Betty. The pair met in 1956 when Barney, his first wife, and two children went to Hampton Beach for vacation and boarded in the same house as Betty. They married five years later in Camden, New Jersey, six years before *Loving v. Virginia* struck down state laws that forbade interracial marriage.[1]

> *It must be a satellite*, he thought as the pancake-shaped disc seemed to follow his Chevrolet Bel Air down US Route 4 near Mt. Pemige-wasset, called Indian Head by locals for its headdress profile. And as the object kept pace, Barney, a World War II veteran, surmised some covert military operation had mistakenly believed the White Mountains would be deserted. But he was uncertain. *What kind of military jet is shaped like that?*[2]

After parking and grabbing his binoculars and pistol, Barney ran into a nearby field to get a closer view of the disc. He stood less than fifty feet away from the glowing object, which was now hovering near the ground, closer than a nearby white pine, and discerned that the craft was piloted: his eyes met those of the occupant. Hysterical, he ran back to the car. By that time, what appeared to be very tall men were standing in the middle of the road, their craft casting a singular light on the highway. Barney was terrified. This blinding fear, a beeping noise, and a sudden daze is the last thing the couple remembers before spotting a sign indicating they were now in Ashland, New Hampshire, thirty-five miles south of where they last recalled being.[3] When the Hills arrived home in Portsmouth later than expected, they discovered that two hours had passed for which they could not account. Neither Barney nor Betty had any immediate recollection of what they would detail in the years to come when prompted to describe their troubling dreams and reflect on that night under hypnosis: tall humanoids with large eyes descended from the sky, dragged them into the woods, and took them captive.

For five consecutive days after the September 19 incident, Betty experienced a series of bizarre nightmares. She would later recall that the dreams were connected to the night at Indian Head.[4] In the following months, Barney's mental and physical health deteriorated. A skeptical man who prided himself on pragmatism, Barney was deeply disturbed by his inability to account for the two hours between Indian Head and Ashland. He developed an ulcer, and his blood pressure rose. In 1962 he developed an undiagnosed series of warts around his groin. Encouraged by his primary physician, Barney and Betty met with Boston psychiatrist Benjamin Simon, former chief of neuropsychiatry at the US Army's Mason General Hospital in December 1962. In separate sessions with Simon, the couple underwent hypnotic regression in the hopes of recalling more complete details of the episode. The Hills alleged that after they were taken aboard the ship, intelligent, methodical beings conducted physical examinations and invasive tests.[5]

While Simon was not convinced that the couple had been abducted by extraterrestrials, he did believe that *they* believed it. Simon wondered whether the couple suffered from folie à deux, or shared psychotic disorder, wherein delusions or hallucinations are transmitted from one person to another, generally between spouses or other family members or from captor to captive.[6] According to the *DSM-II*, social isolation and emotional interdependence were risk factors for the disorder, which is now classified as "induced delusional disorder" in the *ICD-10* (the World Health Organization's classification system) but does not appear in the *DSM-5*. Proponents of this theory take the Hills at their word about the UFO sighting but believe that Barney's recollections of abduction were delusions induced by Betty. Perhaps the pair saw something unusual, but no abduction took place. Or, influenced by Betty's retellings, Barney manufactured a corresponding narrative, creating a circular effect. But because the Hills had no prior history of mental illness and because of the *isolated nature* of the event, Simon never diagnosed them. Instead, he offered his "dream hypothesis." On sighting a UFO, Betty and Barney had become emotionally disoriented. They then had been engulfed by shock during the two hours of "missing time." End of story.[7]

Nevertheless, the couple's allegations captured the imagination of national media outlets and curious citizens when John G. Fuller published his in-depth interview of the couple in *Look* magazine. His 1966 piece, "Aboard a Flying Saucer: The Adventures of Two 'Kidnapped' Humans," is a time capsule of Cold War paranoia. Was the military conducting undisclosed drills or experimenting with new weapons? Were the Soviets using advanced technologies to spy on unsuspecting Americans?[8] Before the Fuller interview, the couple had shared their experience of extraterrestrial encounter only with select friends, relatives, and members of their Unitarian congregation. But after it was published, the Hills catapulted to national fame, theirs the first narrative of an alien abduction in the United States. Betty and Barney became the prototypical abductees or *experiencers*, two terms used to describe people who claim to have had contact with unearthly beings. And their bizarre tale of a Black postal carrier and a white social worker encountering ETs inspired multiple books, films, and TV specials and continues to receive attention in Hollywood.[9]

UFOlogy and Ontology

After Barney's death in 1969, Betty continued recounting the purported events of September 19, 1961, across the globe, delivering keynotes at conventions and conferences, collaborating with investigators, and consulting for projects that capitalized on the couple's allegations. However, despite being the first and only alien abduction experience of a Black American to gain prominence inside and out-side the UFO community, the narrative of Barney Hill remains forgot-ten or neglected by lay investigators and UFOlogists. Likewise, the dissonance evident between the experiences of Barney and Betty, re-vealed in print and audio recordings of the hypnotic regression ses-sions, has been unthought until now. I wanted to contextualize Bar-ney's narrative and account for the "ontological resistance" he lacked as a Black man, a vulnerability that preceded the arrival of space monsters.[10] To put it differently, I wanted to revisit this paranor-mal event with an understanding of abduction as a mundane qual-ity, and the first condition, of Black life. In the process I became versed in UFOlogy—the interdisciplinary investigation of UFOs. Modern UFOlogy is a conglomeration of mostly nongovernmental organiza-tions in the United States and a handful of scholars (predominantly anthropologists, historians, psychologists, and sociologists) docu-menting reports of UFO sightings and attempting to make meaning of UFO abductions. Using varied questions, these communities have arrived at different conclusions. New scientific explanations of the abduction phenomenon have been offered by skeptics over the years. Perhaps these people suffer from "accidental awareness," or the resid-ual trauma of being conscious while anesthetized.[11] Maybe most recount nothing but terrifying bouts of sleep paralysis.[12] Many psy-chologists believe that the phenomenon is a combination of sleep paralysis and shared delusion induced by popular culture, which could even account for this first abduction: weeks before their sight-ing at Indian Head, the Hills had watched an episode of *The Outer Limits* that featured aliens. Meanwhile, historians of American folklore have attempted to determine the cultural function of UFO abduction narratives. Some believe that these narratives stem from America's "first coherent mythical literature"—colonial captivity narratives.[13] These stories of kidnapping, murder, and rape were circulated by colonists to justify their genocidal expansion. Michael Sturma has suggested that these Indian kidnapping narratives share a central metaphor with alien abduction stories—"crossing fronti-ers and the forced experience of another culture."[14] Others have attempted to identify shared perceptions and symbolic practices among abductees. In "Mythmaking in Alien Abduction Narratives,"

Stephanie Kelly-Romano refines the critical distinction between people who have interacted with extraterrestrials (experiencers) and people who are taken against their will (abductees) by analyzing 130 UFO abduction narratives. She organizes all narratives into four categories—physical salvation, hybridization, betterment of humanity, and cosmic humanity—and argues that each one reflects the acculturation and desires of abductees.[15] As I read more and more about the abduction phenomenon, I discovered a confounding absence of Black abductees, save for Barney. If this phenomenon is, as UFO research organizations maintain, truly global and indiscriminate, I wondered, why was every abductee I encountered in the archive—anonymous and named—white? Had not anyone, anywhere asked the same question and uncovered the rhyme or reason? Soon after that, I discovered Lucas Tromly's "Race, Citizenship, and the Politics of Alien Abduction; or, Why Aliens Do Not Abduct Asian Americans." Surely this would offer a theory of the phenomenon that accounted for its homogeneity? "Alien abduction," Tromly writes, "is an inherently *American* experience."[16] He argues that the absence of Asian American abductees proves that the abductee community—"a body of people who stand to be abducted"—is structured by sameness and foreignness. "The racial blind spots of abduction discourse emerge through the difficulty with which Asian Americans, whose conflation of racial and national identities cannot easily be gathered into a fantasy of national sameness, occupy the role of abductee," Tromly writes.[17] Here a person *who stands to be abducted* is not "white" but "American." Tromly notes only one nonwhite abductee—Barney Hill—and calls the American slave narrative the phenomenon's "most important generic precursor." I went looking for Black abductees, but in every study of close encounters I found none. They did not statistically exist, or they remained unaccounted for.[18] I also learned that experiencers are prone to exaggerate the diversity of their communities. According to the website for the Mutual UFO Network (MUFON), a volunteer-based US nonprofit that collects data on sightings and studies abductions worldwide, they receive between five hundred and one thousand reports of sightings every month from a diverse population. But this assertion is unsupported by data. Since the founding of the organization in 1969,

MUFON has never documented the race of experiencers. The director of the organization's California chapter suggested that there was no reason to allow experiencers to report their race when submitting online reports.[19] While this race-blind logic helped explain the whiteness of UFO abduction Reddits and listservs, it didn't explain the absence of abductees in studies. I began to wonder: If the absence of Asian American abductees, according to Tromly, evinced their alienation from national belonging, why were Black American abductees MIA?

Eventually, I read the work of the late psychiatrist and UFOlogy vindicator Dr. John E. Mack. A Harvard University Department of Psychiatry chair and Pulitzer Prize winner, he remains the most eminent scholar to have seriously investigated questions raised by the UFO abduction phenomenon. While his research in child and adolescent psychology and addiction brought him to Harvard, he later became interested in perception and antimaterialism. And after failing, like Benjamin Simon, to pathologize patients recounting abduction experiences, and realizing that no psychogenic cause had ever been identified, Mack commenced a study of two hundred abductees for more than ten years, sixty of whom—all of them white—appear in his 1994 best seller *Abduction: Human Encounters with Aliens*. *Abduction* encourages readers to reconsider the popular assumption that abductees are hoaxers or mentally ill. Instead, Mack takes their experiences seriously. He attends to the absence of preexisting psychological disorders among these patients and highlights their struggle to maintain a sense of well-being or social belonging after their abduction. Mack suggests that studying the phenomenon might enrich our understanding of physical reality. "There are phenomena and experiences reported by abductees," he writes, "for which we can conceive of no explanation within a Newtonian/Cartesian or even Einsteinian space/time ontology."[20] Mack describes the disorientation his patients experience after recalling their purported encounters as the *ontological shock* of abduction: "For until the powerful reliving that has occurred during the hypnosis session, the abductees may have still clung to the possibility that these experiences are dreams or some sort of curable mental disorder."[21] After hypnosis, he discovered, abductees are overwhelmed by the sudden revelation that "their conception of reality does not hold."[22] Troubled, Mack set out to "locate a new ontological ground"—what he imagined might be a parallel dimension or imperceptible space-time—that could account for the claims of his patients.[23]

With Black abductees still nowhere to be found in study after study, the words of Susan Lepselter sound less cryptic and more argumentative. According to Lepselter, those boarded onto alien spacecraft "are immobilized with invisible, uncanny chains; they remind us of other terrors, as they dread leaving their own world and becoming the possessions of these technologically dominating others."[24] What if the absence (or disappearance) of the Black abductee is a problem not of representation, I wondered, but of ontology?

Captivity

Let us begin with a scene of remembering. One is plucked out of bed and floated through the roof of one's home into the hull of a ship, disrobed, prodded, studied, and returned without any explanation or formal recognition. One is reminded of ships carrying ante-human cargo and experiences, ever so briefly: the natal alienation and subjection to the will of another that marked the making of Africans into Blacks and continues to order the Black quotidian. In this way, one might suggest that the abductee unwittingly conspires in the "dethroning" of the human from its "metaphysical pedestal."[25] Surely this recognition speaks to the abductee's humanity. But given that, as Saidiya V. Hartman writes in *Scenes of Subjection*, empathy with the slave "fails to expand the space of the other but merely places the self in its stead," this hypothesis must be problematized.[26]

Recent scholarship in Black studies calls into question the popular assumption that Black life can *be*, unencumbered by the structural violence that initiated and conditions it. Afropessimist thinkers argue that civil society is dependent on anti-Black violence and that this violence cannot be analogized with other regimes that discipline non-Black beings. For Afropessimism, to categorize Black people as human is an epistemological mistake, one that covers a false assumption—"that all sentient beings possess the discursive capacity to transform limitless space into nameable place and endless duration into recognized and incorporated events."[27] Civil society's ontological guarantor is the slave, and the slave's jurisdiction is *the hold*. The hold is not a discrete place but the World. It is not a temporally bound event but the dispersed afterlives of slavery that create and condition Black life. It is the loud and breathing domain of the socially dead. As Christina Sharpe writes, Black people "inhabit and are inhabited by the hold."[28]

When I approached the alien abduction phenomenon as a constitutively white experience, the resonance between the hold and the spaceship became clearer and stronger. Suddenly Mack's theoretical, extradimensional plane appeared a novel invention. How else to shield his patients from the vicious pathology that accompanies any experience with the lacunar "energy of a black, or blackened, position [that] holds out a singularly transformative possibility" for upending human subjectivity?[29] I am suggesting here that a sentient being that is both atomically coherent and ontologically emptied already exists within our known universe. And I am proposing that alien abduction narratives cohere only because of the constitutive, psychosocial disorientation of Black nonbeing. The ontology of alien abduction begins and ends not with a person who *stands to be taken* but with a being who cannot be taken because they *are* not.

Frank B. Wilderson III refers to this sensation as objective vertigo. In *The Vengeance of Vertigo* Wilderson writes:

> Subjective vertigo is vertigo of the event. But the sensation that one is not simply spinning in an otherwise stable environment, that one's environment is perpetually unhinged stems from a relationship to violence that cannot be analogized. This is called objective vertigo, a life constituted by disorientation rather than a life interrupted by disorientation. This is structural as opposed to performative violence. Black subjectivity is a crossroads where vertigoes meet, the intersection of performative and structural violence.[30]

Using Wilderson's grammar, alien abductee experiences are *subjectively vertiginous*. Whether or not the abductee describes the abduction itself as enlightening, frightening, ecstatic, confusing, sensual, or any unmentioned combination, she registers the experience as disorienting because it interrupts the generally self-regulating cognitive map that governs her world. And when she "makes contact" with life that is seemingly not dependent on anti-Black violence, we might call her psychic censure "ontological shock." Still, the abductee encounter is an encounter with, per Wilderson, performative violence. The unauthorized movement of the human *body* through a bedroom window might knock the furry slippers off her feet or leave her neck bruised. But this experience cannot irreparably untether her from *being*—she *will* wake come morning, in bed or perhaps in a field nearby. This anomalous experience will trouble her self-perception, and she may be shunned by others. But spaceman be damned: the abductee stands her ground. The alien abduction phenomenon is not defined by an exposure to subjective violence. What abductees share is an ontological immunity from *objective vertigo*, the structural violence that constitutes Black life before performative violence arrives on the scene in the form of badge, bad guy, or blue-skinned humanoid. To put a finer point on this proposition, let us revisit the story of Barney Hill—a story archivally mute because it illumines "the intersection of performative and structural violence." Barney's narrative of abduction and disorientation is, unlike his wife's, not contingent on spotting a UFO. Indeed, on closer reading, this abduction narrative *is* not. While no complete transcript of Barney's hypnosis has ever been released to the public, verified audio recordings of the sessions made by Simon at the request of the Hills are available on YouTube.[31] In one session Barney begins crying as he recalls approaching the hovering disc. Later, once Barney is more composed, Simon asks him to describe the faces of beings he sees through his binoculars, and he obliges: "It's round. I think of—I think of—a redhead Irishman. . . . I don't know why but . . . I think I know why. Because Irish are usually hostile to Negroes. And when I see a friendly Irish person, I react to him by thinking, 'I will be friendly.' And I think this one that is looking over his shoulder is friendly." About a minute later, after describing the "row of windows" the aliens peer through, Barney adds: "The evil face . . . on the [indecipherable]. . . . He looks like a German Nazi. He is a Nazi. . . . He had a black scarf around his neck, dangling over his left shoulder." It is not uncommon for abductees to project eugenic and physiognomic beliefs onto extraterrestrials they encounter.

Barney initially hesitates to describe the beings as Irish but rationalizes his choice of words aloud: "Because Irish are usually hostile to Negroes." The hostile intentions of the beings watching Barney remind him of the hostility he experiences from his Irish neighbors, the first major immigrant group to settle in New Hampshire. Simon asks whether he recalls where Betty is in this moment and whether he cried out to her. "I'm not close to her," he responds. "I don't know. . . . I don't think of her." Later Barney tells Simon that he felt "like a rabbit" and provides the following explanation: "I was hunting for rabbits in Virginia. And this cute little bunny went into a bush that was not very big. . . . And the poor little bunny thought he was safe. . . . He was just hiding behind a little stalk which meant security to him, when I pounced on him, and captured the poor little bunny who thought he was safe. Funny I thought of that. Right there out in the field. I felt like a rabbit." One hundred sixty-five years before this night, a fifteen-minute walk from the Hills' Portsmouth home, Senator John Langdon saw to it that enslaved fugitive Oney Judge learned that Burwell Bassett, the nephew of George Washington, had been sent by the family to capture her and return her to Mount Vernon. Each attempt to abduct the Black woman and return her to her important owners promised to end her pursuit of freedom. When Judge died in 1848, Barney's great-grandmother, the daughter of a white plantation owner, might have been alive. She too would have been subject to what Calvin L. Warren has described as the "onto-metaphysical instability" that kidnappers and their accomplices exploited for profit. Warren also reminds us that this enterprise of capture was about more than monetary reward: "Kidnapping relies on the precarious Black self—since this self exists to not exist, it is fleeting and material. Kidnapping illustrates that the free Black does not exist as human being, since the ontological presumptions of freedom are denied blacks."[32] In identifying with the "poor little bunny" he preys on, Barney meditates on the violable nature of his freedom, even more precarious than the perceived safety of the bunny hiding behind a bush too small to conceal his presence. While the rabbit's vulnerability is conditional—he could survive Barney were the bush larger or his body smaller—Barney's exposure to gratuitous violence is unconditional. His relation to being is one of captivity, and in this field, a metal disc hovering above, he finds himself "available in the *flesh immediate . . .* hands on."[33] As he recounts his experience, Barney becomes increasingly emotional.

> I know this creature, this leader is telling me something . . . I can see it in his face . . . his lips aren't moving . . . but he's looking at me . . . "Stay there and keep looking, just keep looking and stay there and just keep looking . . . just keep looking . . ." Oh, I gotta pull these binoculars away from my eyes! Because if I don't I'll just keep staying there! . . . "Just stay there," he's saying to me. It's pounding in my head! Pull the binoculars away! God give me strength! Pull 'em down! RUN! PULL THE BINOCULARS DOWN AND RUN! IF THERE'S A GOD GIVE ME STRENGTH![34]

At this point in the session Barney breaks out in hysterics, screaming and sobbing as he tries to catch his breath. Simon would later share that he worried Barney would jump out of the office window. And though Simon begins consoling Barney, assuring him that he cannot be harmed, Barney begs: "Those eyes: they're in my brain. Please, can I wake up?" Fanon identifies this ocular assault in *Black Skin, White Masks*: "I am being dissected under white eyes, the only real eyes. I am fixed. Having adjusted their microtomes, they objectively cut away slices of my reality. I am laid bare." And when Barney wakes, he will wake again to find himself "in the world . . . an object in the midst of other objects."[35]

If, as Warren suggests, the denial of freedom to Blacks "provides the condition of possibility for kidnapping," this denial also provides the condition of *impossibility* for Barney's nonabduction. The Black abductee's "subsumption by objective vertigo . . . unique to his paradigmatic position" prevents his account from registering as a physical *or* psychogenic encounter because, as Wilderson suggests, "Black political ontology is foreclosed in the unconscious just as it is foreclosed in the court."[36] Thus Barney, the inaugural abductee, fails to *be* an abductee proper. If the alien abduction phenomenon is an experientially inaccessible domain for the Black nonsubject, then the figuration of the cosmos as a refuge for Blackness is cause for concern. And it may be that by investigating the qualities of other paranormal phenomena, we can more readily internalize the possibility that no law will endure the cosmic destruction our freedom requires.

As I contemplate how to steady my own hands and hold closer the binoculars quivering in my own sweaty palms, what I see terrifies me. I cannot look away.

....

JONATHAN JACOB MOORE is a PhD student in the Department of African American and African Diaspora Studies at the University of California, Berkeley. He studies the relationship between Afropessimism and Black feminist theories of the human, poetics, and the paranormal. He hosts the monthly Black politics and culture podcast *abolitionISH*.

Notes

1. Marden and Friedman, *Captured!*
2. YouTube, "Barney Hill Hypnosis—Complete."
3. Marden and Friedman, *Captured!*, 111.
4. Marden and Friedman, *Captured!*, 84.
5. Fuller, "Aboard a Flying Saucer."
6. Benjamin Simon to Philip J. Klass, March 1, 1976, Betty and Barney Hill Papers, 1961–2006, Milne Special Collections and Archives, Dimond Library, University of New Hampshire.
7. In the years after Barney's death in 1969, Simon ultimately admitted that he believed that the stress of being in an interracial marriage and Barney's "racial paranoia" had led the Hills to unconsciously materialize an unbelievable narrative, revealing only their long-standing anxieties and fears. See Simon to Klass.
8. Fuller, "Aboard a Flying Saucer."
9. Weiss, "New Docu-series."
10. Fanon, *Black Skin, White Masks*, 83.
11. Forrest, "Alien Abduction," 432.
12. McNally and Clancy, "Sleep Paralysis."
13. Slotkin, *Regeneration through Violence*, 95.
14. Sturma, "Aliens and Indians," 321.
15. Kelley-Romano, "Mythmaking in Alien Abduction Narratives," 391–402.
16. Tromly, "Race, Citizenship, and the Politics of Alien Abduction," 276. My emphasis.
17. Tromly, "Race, Citizenship, and the Politics of Alien Abduction," 277.
18. Bader, "Supernatural Support Groups."

19. Ruben Uriarte, unpublished interview by author, October 2018.
20. Mack, *Abduction Human Encounters with Aliens*, 46.
21. Mack, *Abduction Human Encounters with Aliens*, 11.
22. Mack, *Abduction Human Encounters with Aliens*, 140.
23. Kastrup, *Meaning in Absurdity*.
24. Lepselter, *Resonance of Unseen Things*, 67.
25. Warren, *Ontological Terror*, 23.
26. Hartman, *Scenes of Subjection*, 9.
27. Douglass, Terrefe, and Wilderson, "Afro-pessimism."
28. Sharpe, *In the Wake*, 138.
29. Sexton, "Afro-pessimism."
30. Wilderson, "Vengeance of Vertigo."
31. See YouTube, "Barney Hill Hypnosis—Complete." All quotations of Barney's words in this paragraph are taken from this source.
32. Warren, *Ontological Terror*, 107.
33. Hortense J. Spillers speaking in Arthur Jafa's film *Dreams Are Colder Than Death*.
34. YouTube, "Barney Hill Hypnosis—Complete."
35. Fanon, *Black Skin, White Masks*, 87, 82.
36. Wilderson, *Afropessimism*, 30.

References

American Psychiatric Association. *Diagnostic and Statistical Manual of Mental Disorders*. 2nd ed. Washington, DC: American Psychiatric Association, 1968.

American Psychiatric Association. *Diagnostic and Statistical Manual of Mental Disorders*. 5th ed. Washington, DC: American Psychiatric Association, 2013.

Bader, Christopher D. "Supernatural Support Groups: Who Are the UFO Abductees and Ritual-Abuse Survivors?" *Journal for the Scientific Study of Religion* 42, no. 4 (2003): 669–78.

Douglass, Patrice, Selamawit D. Terrefe, and Frank B. Wilderson. "Afro-pessimism." Oxford University Press, August 28, 2018. doi.org/10.1093/obo/9780190280024-0056.

Fanon, Frantz. *Black Skin, White Masks*, translated by Charles Lam Markmann. London: Pluto, 2008.

Forrest, David V. "Alien Abduction: A Medical Hypothesis." *Journal of the American Academy of Psychoanalysis and Dynamic Psychiatry* 36, no. 3 (2008): 431–42.

Fuller, John G. "Aboard a Flying Saucer: The Adventures of Two 'Kidnapped' Humans." *Look Magazine*, October 4, 1966, 45–56.

Hartman, Saidiya V. *Scenes of Subjection: Terror, Slavery, and Self-Making in Nineteenth-Century America*. New York: Oxford University Press, 1997.

Jafa, Arthur, dir. *Dreams Are Colder Than Death*. Independent, 2014.

Kastrup, Bernardo. *Meaning in Absurdity: What Bizarre Phenomena Can Tell Us about the Nature of Reality*. Winchester: Iff Books, 2011.

Kelley-Romano, Stephanie. "Mythmaking in Alien Abduction Narratives." *Communication Quarterly* 54, no. 3 (2006): 383–406.

Lepselter, Susan Claudia. *The Resonance of Unseen Things: Poetics, Power, Captivity, and UFOs in the American Uncanny*. Ann Arbor: University of Michigan Press, 2016.

Mack, John. *Abduction Human Encounters with Aliens*. Bertrams Print On Demand, 2007. www.vlebooks.com/vleweb/product/openreader?id =none&isbn=9781439190029.

Marden, Kathleen, and Stanton T. Friedman. *Captured! The Betty and Barney Hill UFO Experience: The True Story of the World's First Documented Alien Abduction*. Franklin Lakes, NJ: New Page, 2007.

McNally, Richard J., and Susan A. Clancy. "Sleep Paralysis, Sexual Abuse, and Space Alien Abduction." *Transcultural Psychiatry* 42, no. 1 (2005): 113–22.

Sexton, Jared. "Afro-pessimism: The Unclear Word." *Rhizomes: Cultural Studies in Emerging Knowledge*, no. 29 (2016). doi.org/10.20415/rhiz/ 029.e02.

Sharpe, Christina. *In the Wake: On Blackness and Being*. Durham, NC: Duke University Press, 2016.

Slotkin, Richard. *Regeneration through Violence: The Mythology of the American Frontier, 1600–1860*. Norman: University of Oklahoma Press, 2000.

Sturma, Michael. "Aliens and Indians: A Comparison of Abduction and Captivity Narratives." *Journal of Popular Culture* 36, no. 2 (2002): 318–34.

Tromly, Lucas. "Race, Citizenship, and the Politics of Alien Abduction; or, Why Aliens Do Not Abduct Asian Americans." *Journal of Popular Culture* 50, no. 2 (2017): 276–92.

Warren, Calvin L. *Ontological Terror: Blackness, Nihilism, and Emancipation*. Durham, NC: Duke University Press, 2018.

Weiss, Josh. "New Docu-series Explores How Betty and Barney Hill Changed UFO Culture with Their Famous Story of Alien Abduction." *SyFy*, August 25, 2021. www.syfy.com/syfy-wire/betty-barney-hill-ufo -showtime.

Wilderson, Frank B., III. *Afropessimism*. New York: Liveright, 2020.

Wilderson, Frank B., III. "The Vengeance of Vertigo: Aphasia and Abjection in the Political Trials of Black Insurgents." *InTensions*, no. 5 (2011). www.yorku.ca/intent/issue5/articles/pdfs/frankbwildersoniiiarticle.pdf.

World Health Organization. *International Statistical Classification of Diseases and Related Health Problems (ICD)*. 10th ed. Geneva: World Health Organization, 2019.

YouTube. "Barney Hill Hypnosis—Complete." Posted December 19, 2012. www.youtube.com/watch?v=TNGOaSGVwDg.

Keep up to date on new scholarship

Issue alerts are a great way to stay current on all the cutting-edge scholarship from your favorite Duke University Press journals. This free service delivers tables of contents directly to your inbox, informing you of the latest groundbreaking work as soon as it is published.

To sign up for issue alerts:

1. Visit **dukeu.press/register** and register for an account. You do not need to provide a customer number.

2. After registering, visit **dukeu.press/alerts**.

3. Go to "Latest Issue Alerts" and click on "Add Alerts."

4. Select as many publications as you would like from the pop-up window and click "Add Alerts."

read.dukeupress.edu/journals

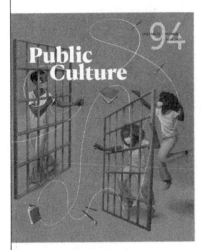